M.A.D. About Sweets
Bake My Cake and Eat It Too!

"For I know the plans I have for you, declares the Lord, plans to prosper you and not harm you, plans to give you hope and a future." - Jeremiah 29:11

M.A.D. About Sweets: Bake My Cake and Eat It Too!
Copyright © 2018 by Marsha Adele Davis

All rights reserved. No part of this book may be reproduced, scanned, or distributed in any printed or electronic form without permission.
First Edition: April 2018
Printed in the United States of America

Editors:
Traneisha Jones and Rosalind Spells

Co-Editor:
Terra Knight

Principle Photographer:
Jacqueline Amparo
Photographer and Artist, Jacqueline Amparo Photography
Website: www.jamparo.com
Phone: (760) 342-8212

Published by:

Best Hands Management, Incorporated
Best Hands Publishing
Speak Life, Make It Happen, Live With Purpose
P.O. Box 394
Normal, IL 61761
Email: besthandsmanagement@gmail.com

This book is dedicated to the memory of my maternal grandmother, Grandma Cal. Without her I wouldn't have discovered the joy and possibilities of baking and cooking. With heart, soul, hardwork, and a whole lot of prayer, M.A.D. About Sweets would not have been possible.

Acknowledgments

My entire life I've been surrounded by family and friends who've instilled in me a portion of their artistic abilities, and the joy of baking and cooking. These individuals laid the foundation for me to succeed. I have respect for their journey, spiritual guidance, patience, and unconditional love, for without it, this project would not be possible.

To my mother, Margaret Davis, whose prayers have guided me from the day I was born. The doctor's told her to feed me so I could gain weight or else I wouldn't make it. God had plans for me and he used my mom and food to start me off in the right direction.

Clarice Davis, my sister and friend, growing up was an adventure. Our dreams as children were fulfilled when we played with paper dolls that we made from catalog models, hoping and praying that our lives would be far better as adults. My sister has been there for every minor and major event in my life, and for that I'm forever grateful.

Paul D. Roberts, my cousin, we clicked from the moment we met seventeen years ago, and we've been close ever since. Your compassion, support, and encouragement have carried me through some tough times. I'm thankful for your friendship and kind words written for the foreword.

Danielle Bolden, my cousin, and a fellow baker and cook who supplied photographs of our grandmother, Carolyn Sanderson, which brought this book together.

To Uncle Danny who encouraged me to continue doing God's work by writing this book and making fabulous food.

To my best friend, Rosalind Spells, who has been my supporter from the first day we met in August 1987. Our connection as friends felt like a soul-sister that I didn't know existed. No matter the challenges, heartache, and problems we've encountered, we have always been there for one another. Rosalind, my prayer partner, soul-sister, and best friend, my life is forever filled with joy because of your presence.

Mr. Morris Hayes, our friendship has spanned more than thirty-four years, which started as a spiritual and musical meeting that forever changed my life. Your talent as a musician, keyboard player, composer, writer, and singer have inspired me to explore my God-given talents. Your perseverance over the years made me want to do more, be more, create more, and to be better today than I was yesterday. Your fearless attitude, humility, grace, support, and prayers lifted me up when I didn't think I could go any further. I'm abundantly grateful for your prayers, wisdom, sense of humor, and friendship.

My friend and soul-sister Terra Knight, you are the epitome of love and encouragement. Our friendship started out at Sears in Ford City Mall in Chicago, and the dynamics of our friendship made people wonder and want what we had. We just clicked. Your prophetic abilities have changed my life, and I'm absolutely grateful for your friendship, support, and prayers while on this journey.

Huge thank you to my friend and the photographer responsible for many of the images in this book, Jacqueline Amparo, for making me and the food look amazing. Jacqueline, you have an eye for finding the beauty in everything. Thank you for capturing the beauty in me and the food I prepared.

Secondly to Sherman Hackett, thank you for stepping in as my back-up photographer. Your presence was calming, and you were able to adjust your schedule to my specifications. The experience kept me on my toes.

To a host of other friends who have encouraged me through this process: Andrea Jaouhari, Nicole Trimble, Gina Carey, Andrea (Dr. Tian's office), Victoria Perkins, Seleste, Candi Hawk, and Leslie & Mitchell (from Champion Life Church). I appreciate you all.

Last but not least, to my son, Myles Davis, my dessert taste tester from the age of one. If something doesn't taste right, you'll tell me what it needs to make it pop. You're my constant supporter and I'm grateful to be your mother.

Special Thanks

I met James Schend, Food Editor of *Taste of Home Magazine* via email over two years ago after my recipe for 7-Up Pound Cake was chosen as an Honorable Mention in the February/March 2015 issue of *Taste of Home Magazine*. Initially I thought it was spam mail, but my son insisted that I read the email before deleting it, so I did. I responded to the email, and the next thing I knew, I was submitting photos, answering a questionnaire about my passion for baking, and appearing on the Hallmark Home & Family Show.

My passion for baking has come full circle, and transformed into a cookbook. I told James I was writing a cookbook, and if he could offer me any advice for a successful first cookbook what would it be. He said, "Since this is your first cookbook, you want it done right, and it is probably best to research publishing companies. Your first cookbook should done by a professional because it has your name on it." And I've been reaching out to James on occasion ever since. I consider James Schend a faraway mentor because he knows food and has an eye for details. Thank you James for encouraging me to pursue this out of the box idea of writing my first cookbook. Your knowledge of the culinary world has helped me tremendously.

Ranis Thomas, your insight about publishing my book has given me a broader view of what to expect before, during, and after my book is published. Thank you for the tips, suggestions, opinions, and encouragement to keep pushing forward no matter how long it takes. Your journey to become an author inspired me to continue even when I wanted to give up. Thank you for taking time out of your full schedule to tell me the truth about the process, and that it would be worth it in the end when my book is online and on the shelves of Barnes & Noble.

Positive Praise from Family & Friends

My sister is M.A.D. About Sweets in a special way. She has the gift of baking all types of desserts from scratch. You can actually taste and know they are from her heart, which is a heart of gold. It shows everywhere she goes, while traveling place to place. She glows everywhere. And she deserves the best in everything. My prayer is for her to continue to grow while she glows every day of her life. - Clarice Monee Davis

My dear friend is as sweet as they come and has a passion for baking and cooking. She has a gift of expression through her tasty inventions as we are all so blessed to enjoy the fruits of her labor. She is a one in a million friend. I'm so happy to see her bloom in this season of her life. She is a true treasure! - Andrea Jaouhari

Please do not pass on the opportunity to explore a succulent dish that hugs your taste buds. *M.A.D About Sweets* offers cuisine that reaches beyond satisfying one's sweet tooth, it is cuisine that connects with the soul. Marsha's culinary talent vibrantly comes to life in each dish that is lovingly prepared and tailored to complement your individual dietary needs. Awaken your spirit with *M.A.D. About Sweets*! - Terra Knight

Anything Marsha says or does is done with love. Every dessert she has made I've eaten and it has been wonderful! She is an amazing person, mother, and friend! - Chris Morris

Marsha is wonderful and as sweet as the German Chocolate Cake she baked for me. She's a great friend and has a beautiful spirit. - Rosalind Spells

My daughter's Red Velvet Cake and Caramel Cake melt in your mouth. All of her cakes are delicious! - Margaret Crenshaw

I feel a sense of euphoria every time I take a bite of my mom's cakes, apple pies, cookies, or some dessert concoction. I've enjoyed most desserts my mother makes, especially after realizing how wonderful they taste. - Myles Davis

The three words I would use to describe Marsha's butter cookies are Dee-li-cious! Marsha is kind, humble, conscientious, compassionate, has great energy, and is passionate about her craft. She is a classy lady. - Morris Hayes

The Red Velvet cake was moist and the sour cream frosting was sweet and tart at the same time. The sweetness of the frosting paired well with the cake. It reminded me of a carrot cake, but with a twist. The beet powder added an interesting level of spice to the cake. It was delicious! - Angela M.

Marsha's 7-Up Pound Cake is so delicious, light and moist, with a burst of lemon flavor. It's by far one of my favorite cakes. - Nicki Trimble

I'm not much of a cake eater, but Marsha's 7-Up Pound Cake was lemony, moist, and just sweet enough for me to enjoy. - Delphina

Table of Contents

Foreword..................................i
Preface..................................ii
Introduction..............................I
Part I: Desserts..........................5
Part 2: Breakfast Time...................28
Part 3: Knight (Night) Time..............37
Part 4: Fill-In Meals & Sides............44
Part 5: Sandwiches & Burgers.............53
Part 6: Salads...........................63
Before I Do (Resources)..................69

Foreword

Before you move to the first chapter of this cookbook, brace yourself, you are in for a real treat! This cookbook was uniquely crafted with you in mind. Whether you are a newbie or you know your way around the kitchen, this cookbook is perfect for you. It offers traditional and new recipes with natural ingredients that are tailored to fit your lifestyle and dietary needs. You are what you eat, and the author, Marsha A. Davis, wants you to feel good about what you eat.

Having the ability to prepare baked goods and home cooked meals is a true talent. Marsha discovered her love of baking at age eight, but learned her first real recipe at age 10. Her grandmother and mother's kitchens were transformed into a training station, which gave her room to sharpen her culinary skills. Marsha was given the opportunity to learn how to bake cakes, cookies, pies, macaroni and cheese, and much more. As the aroma of delicious food filled their homes, Marsha's family was eager to try her new creations; and with their support and feedback, she was able to perfect signature dishes that she serves today.

Each and every recipe shared in this cookbook is a piece of Marsha's soul, as her charisma, laughter, and vivaciousness are poured in every signature dish and dessert. While the ingredients of the recipes will tug at your taste buds, they will also comfort your spirit and leave you feeling like home. Marsha is a talented culinary expert with a niche in bringing family and friends together. Adding this cookbook to your collection will warm your heart and leave your mouth watering for more. Enjoy!

Terra Knight

Foreword

I count it an honor and a privilege to be asked to write the foreword for *M.A.D. About Sweets: Bake My Cake and Eat It Too!* I am certain you will find this book delightful, with many wonderful recipes for healthy and delicious dishes. I am excited for this opportunity for you and pray for your success!

Paul D. Roberts

Preface

M. A. D. About Sweets: Bake My Cake and Eat It Too! started off as a romance novel. I wanted to delve right in with juicy details of romance, but I soon realized I didn't have a clue about romance. I asked myself what is romance? And why am I writing about something I've only read about? Don't get me wrong, I've had romantic encounters with that special someone, but writing a story about two people on their journey to romance and love wasn't going to happen. I was determined to finish what I started, so I started writing again. After a discussion with my aunt, Carrie and son, Myles, it dawned on me that I didn't have to write a story about a romantic relationship between a man and a woman, I could write about my relationship with food. A baking-cooking relationship; a passionate relationship and how it began. So I prayed and God answered. The words poured out of me as if I was pouring glaze on my 7-Up Pound Cake. *Enjoy!*

Introduction

If you're reading this passage, you've embarked on my *M.A.D. About Sweets: Bake My Cake and Eat it Too!* journey by purchasing this cookbook. Thank you for coming along with me to learn how it all started. This cookbook was a labor of love that I really hadn't planned on writing until I had a conversation with my son, Myles, and a confirming conversation with my aunt, Carrie. Needless to say, I'm humbled by this experience. The research, writing, and doing my best to remember important details that played a key role in my development in becoming a baker and home cook has been hectic, but worth it. Everyone has a relationship with food, but it's our perception of food that makes our journey unique. Initially this book began as a fairy tale romance novel that I started writing five years ago. I wanted to write something profound, but I couldn't find my voice so I allowed the book idea to rest until I figured out what the Holy Spirit wanted me to say. I prayed and God answered. In December 2015, I opened up the computer, erased what I had written (the romance stuff), and began to type. I found my voice in the midst of health issues and uncertainty about the direction of my life, and where this book would take me. I reached down in my soul and took ahold of my destiny that had been there all along. I believe this wonderful journey of self-discovery, or really rediscovery, was a romance of sorts. It was a romance with my food and passion for baking that brought a sense of joy and peace. The words flowed from my heart through my fingers just like when I bake a dessert or prepare a dish. God spoke through my soul and *M. A. D. About Sweets: Bake My Cake and Eat It Too* was born.

Everyone has a story that comes with a few bumps in the road, but I wouldn't have grown into the person I am today without them. You see, Grandma Carolyn and my dad, Clarence, actually taught me how to bake and cook. I learned by watching and listening to the spoken and unspoken words in the kitchen. Not only was I inspired by my grandmother and dad, but I also found inspiration by watching Julia Child and Rick Bayless on PBS, and Rachel Ray, and Paula Deen on The Food Network, seeing other home cooks and chefs prepare dishes, and reading cookbooks. I fell in love with three completely different chefs, but I was particularly drawn to Paula Dean because of her back-story of struggling as a wife and mother, and then a divorcee raising two boys on her own. I too am a single parent and wanted to succeed in the baking industry as she had. Paula started out a little late, but look at her now. My grandmother and dad didn't gain notoriety, fame, and fortune by their culinary skills, but to the family they were famous in their own right. As I recollect over my life I realize that my culinary journey was inevitable because of them. It's in my DNA. I pray that as you prepare the recipes in this cookbook, you'll make wonderful memories with your family and friends too.

Bake My Cake and Eat It Too!

Bake my cake and eat it too is about a relationship between me and you.
A journey of self-discovery; embracing the old, welcoming the new.
I sat in the kitchen and realized this is my place to become who I was created to be,
To see you staring back at me in awe.
The ingredients on the counter ready to come together to become something special,
Not just batter or cake, but completion, a purpose.

Bake my cake and eat it too is about a relationship between me and you.
A journey of self discovery-joy, pain, sorrow, and peace.
To experience life with passion in motion and standing still at the same time.

Bake my cake and eat it too is about a relationship between me and you.
A journey of self discovery, being at the right place at the right time.
Seeing the fruits of my labor and enjoying the ride.

Let's Bake A Cake

*I have a sweet tooth that I can't seem to shake
so I figured I would just bake a cake.
I close my eyes to imagine what dessert I will create.
Then I slowly open my eyes to find the kitchen
cabinets open as the ingredients jump from the
shelves onto the counter, speaking to my hands and heart.
From shelf to counter to an oven is my goal, baking
a cake comes straight from my soul.*

Part 1:
Let's Bake A Cake

Desserts

7-Up Pound Cake | Orange Soda Cake | Banana Pudding Cake | My Sweet Baby's Carrot Cake
Red Velvet Cake | Lemon- Lime Ginger Cheesecake Parfaits | Pear Cobbler
Apple Pecan Crumble Pie | M.A.D. About Sweets Butter Cookie

M.A.D. About Sweets
Bake My Cake and Eat It Too!

Once upon a time there was a girl named Marsha who lived in a magic kingdom full of love, peace, fairies, and baked goodies galore. At every turn whatever Marsha touched, turned into delicious desserts. All kinds of wonderful things would occur. Marsha loved her magic kingdom very much but there had to be more to the kingdom that she was yet to discover. Wait just a darn minute. What happened? I must've fallen asleep. Who doesn't love a good fairy tale, but that's a bit much. A magic kingdom? Really? Hmmmm... This is how the story really goes. I was born and raised in Chicago a.k.a. the Windy City or Chi Town. I enjoyed living in Chicago. I experienced normalcy and had a close-knit family that consisted of my grandmother, Carolyn Sanderson, my parents, my sister- Clarice, my Auntie Debbie and host of other aunts, uncles, and cousins.

My childhood activities consisted of reading, writing poetry, listening to music, watching T.V. and daydreaming (obvious from the introduction), and using my Easy Bake Oven to make miniature cake delights. I was shy and felt a little awkward. I was most comfortable spending time by myself when I wasn't spending time with my sister and friend, Clarice or in the kitchen absorbing all I could until given a chance to do more. I did well in school, which became a wonderful pastime. You see, when you're good or great at something, it doesn't take much effort, or so I thought. Even though I succeeded academically, I still felt like I needed something else. I desired something more and I received it at age ten when my Grandma Carolyn gave me a special gift that I would treasure for the rest of my life, a recipe for 7-Up Pound Cake. She took it out of her recipe box and handed it to me. I felt like I had just won an Academy Award. Time stood still and I was humbled that my grandmother loved me enough to entrust me with such a special gift. All that time baking with my Easy Bake Oven wasn't in vain after all. Little did I know this was just the beginning of my designed purpose.

7-Up Pound Cake

This is my first real cake recipe, gifted to me by my Grandmother Carolyn.

3 Cups Unbleached All-Purpose Flour
3 Cups Pure Cane Sugar (Can also use white sugar, which is what I used until 2009)
3 Sticks Organic Butter, Room Temperature (Can also use Earth Balance Buttery Sticks)
5 Large Eggs, Room Temperature (Cage Free)
3/4 Cup 7-Up or Sierra Mist (I now use Organic Sparkling Lemonade)
2 Tablespoons Fresh Lemon Juice or Pure Lemon Extract
1 Teaspoon Pure Vanilla Extract

Lemon Glaze

1 1/2 Cups Confectioners Sugar
1 Tablespoon Lemon Juice
1 to 2 Tablespoons 7-Up (Can also use Organic Lemon-Lime Pure Cane Soda or Sparkling Lemonade)
1/2 Teaspoon Grated Lemon and Lime Zest (Optional)

Recipe Continued On Next Page

Alternative Lemon Glaze

1/2 Cup Water
1/2 Cup Pure Cane Sugar
1 Tablespoon Fresh Lemon Juice
2 Tablespoons 7-Up or Sierra Mist (Organic Lemon-Lime Soda or Sparkling Lemonade)
1 Cup Powder Sugar
1/2 Teaspoon Grated Lemon Zest (Optional)

Preparation: Preheat the oven to 350 degrees. Grease and flour a 10-inch fluted or bundt cake pan. In a large bowl, cream the butter and sugar until light and fluffy. Add eggs one at a time, beating well after each addition. Beat in lemon juice and vanilla extract. Add flour alternately with 7-Up, beginning and ending with flour, beating well after each addition. Be careful not to overbeat batter. Bake for 60 to 75 minutes or until a toothpick comes out clean. While cake is baking in a medium bowl, mix the ingredients for the glaze, and set aside until cake is done baking. Remove cake from the oven, and allow cake to stand in pan for 10 to 15 minutes. Turn cake onto a cake plate to continue to cool. Pour glaze over cooled cake. *Cut, serve and enjoy.*

Looking back over my life, I realize I've always enjoyed the process of baking desserts. I received my first Easy Bake Oven when I was six or seven years old, and I used that oven until I couldn't use it anymore. I was mesmerized by the aroma of sweetness that filled my nostrils as well as the decorating details on the cakes and pies in the grocery store bakery my mom, sister and I would visit. I would think to myself, "One day I'll be making and decorating cakes like that." At this point I wanted to graduate to something bigger, and receiving the 7-Up Pound Cake recipe from my grandmother was like graduating. It changed me emotionally and spiritually. Grandma Carolyn and I shared a special moment as we went into the kitchen, and step-by-step she showed me how the magic happened from bowl to oven. It was my grandmother and my parents who introduced me to the world of baking, cooking, and the church. They laid the foundation to my Christian life. I wanted to honor God with my life by using my gifts, talents and abilities.

" I am reminded of your sincere faith that dwelt first in your grandmother Lois and your mother Eunice and now, I am sure, dwells in you as well." - 2 Timothy 1:5

I felt special in that moment and every time I bake a 7-Up Pound Cake or anything else for that matter, I think of that extraordinary day. Grandma Cal is what we called Grandmother Carolyn. Not only did she show me how to bake this cake, but she also showed me how to bake and cook many delicious desserts and meals including; squash pie, sweet potato pie, steaks, pork chops, macaroni and cheese, cornbread dressing, and perfect scrambled eggs. She even showed me how to make rice. I carefully watched how she meticulously arranged her food in the kitchen in her apartment on 79th & Loomis. No matter what she made, it came out great. Grandma Cal didn't measure when she cooked unless she was baking. Her measurement style included a hand full of this, and pinches of that. She used the eyeball method. Grandma Cal had been cooking for so long it was second nature. I wanted to find my own groove in the kitchen, and my mode of expression, but I still wanted her finesse while baking and cooking any feast.

" For seven days celebrate the Feast to the Lord your God at the place the Lord will choose. For the Lord your God will bless you in all your harvest and in all the work of your hands, and your joy will be complete." - Deuteronomy 16:15

We all have something special from our past that makes up who we are and what we'll become. My dad didn't give me any recipes per se, but he showed me his style of cooking. He baked too, but his main talent was cooking and grilling the best barbecue I ever ate. He made the best ribs and chicken on that grill. It melted in your mouth at first bite. He definitely knew his way around a kitchen, but grilling was his domain. Family and friends would travel far to partake of his barbecue goodness. My dad taught me the how and what of mastering the grill, but I fancied an oven style barbecue because it felt more ladylike (my quirky thinking).

While the ribs, rib tips, and chicken did its thing on the grill, I sat next to my dad absorbing and appreciating the moment as I received cooking and life lessons rolled into one. I observed my dad, Clarence Davis, listening to music while he cooked and grilled. Now I sometimes find myself listening to music and even singing while I bake or cook, but I prefer silence and most of the time when music is playing or the television is on while I'm in the kitchen, I don't hear a thing.

While doing an interview with the cast of the Hallmark Home & Family Show, I was asked a question, "What is baking to you?" I answered, "Baking has been and is my therapy. It relaxes me when I'm stressed, overwhelmed and underwhelmed. Baking and cooking brings a smile to my face."

As Suzanne Goin says in her introduction to *The A.O.C. Cookbook*, "Learning to cook really is similar to learning another language. You have to do it rigorously, practice, and pay attention. Every time you cook, it is a chance to learn and take away a lesson."

As soon as I enter the kitchen and start measuring the ingredients, I feel like I'm in another world. My soul and spirit come alive, and a sense of being present and at peace consumes me.

Photo Courtesy of TasteofHome.com

" My soul will be satisfied as with the richest of foods; with singing lips my mouth will praise you." - Psalm 63:5

I realized after baking cakes and various desserts for family functions, I wanted to do something with my talent, but I wasn't sure what direction I should take. In seventh grade, I started a small cake business, but not without a few bumps in the road (I had a lot of those too) which ultimately allowed me to grow as a self-taught baker. I figured I would apply to culinary school and become a pastry chef, but my plans were thwarted and I went in a different direction. Instead I earned a degree in business management, a degree I don't regret receiving, but it wasn't what I had envisioned for myself. As years passed, I continued baking for special events- birthday parties, wedding and bridal showers, and even homegoings, just because I could. If I can bring a smile to someone's face by baking them a cake or dessert of their choice, I've done my job. I'm here to serve those whom God places in my path.

" Each of you should use whatever gift you have received to serve others as faithful stewards of God's grace in its various forms." - 1 Peter 4:10

Usually when a person is deciding a career path, fame and fortune are at the top of the list. Fame is good in some respects, but it was not my ultimate goal. I wanted to honor God by learning as much as I could, and still have fun. My dad said it didn't matter what my career choice was, as long as I lived a happy and fulfilled life.

He said, " *Pursue your dreams with passion because you only have one life.*"

I thank God every day for blessing me with a passion for baking and cooking, and for choosing my grandmother to light the way and my father to reinforce it.

I hope and pray I've made my grandmother and dad proud by pursuing my passion for baking- turning on the oven, measuring the ingredients, and watching the creation rise in the oven.

I've always had a relationship with food- good, bad, and indifferent. I overindulged on food, mostly sweets, as a comfort and as an escape when I was upset about something that happened in my life. I needed to take that negative energy and rechannel the energy for something positive, and well, baking was that something. With help from my grandma, dad, and two aunts, feelings of inadequacy dissipated, and over time I learned to love myself as much as I love baking. I used that energy to create goodness in the kitchen.

" Help my children develop a strong self-esteem that is rooted in the realization that they are God's workmanship created in Christ Jesus. " - Ephesians 2:10

Baking and cooking was a great way for me to extend my interest into other culinary fields- catering and event planning. I have since baked my way into several recipe contests, and my 7- Up Pound Cake recipe was featured in the February/March 2015 issue of *Taste of Home Magazine*. When I received the email telling me of this honorable mention, I felt like that ten-year-old girl when my Grandmother Carolyn handed me the recipe. It is a moment I will treasure as long as I have breath in my body.

As I embark on a career in baking, I realize this journey is filled with trials and surprises of many sorts, but I'm willing to succumb to the challenge.

" Let us not become weary in doing good, for at the proper time we will reap a harvest if we do not give up." - Galatians 6:9

Desserts

I've created a few recipes over the years, and one of those recipes is the Orange Soda Cake. After teaching me the ins and outs of baking and cooking, my Grandma Cal decided to be adventerous and bake an orange pound cake in the microwave. It was a lovely sight to see, but it didn't sit well with my stomach. Needless to say, she never baked another cake in the microwave, and continued her awesome baking in a conventional oven. After that experience, I was a little apprehensive about eating any dessert made with oranges even though I enjoy eating the fruit.

Years later, as I was embarking on yet another cake recipe contest for *Woman's Magazine*, I created an orange soda bundt cake. I had fun making it, but then I discovered I could turn my 7-Up Pound Cake into a wonderful orange delight.

Orange Soda Cake

3 Cups Unbleached All-Purpose Flour
3 Cups Organic Pure Cane Sugar
3 Sticks Unsalted Butter, Room Temperature
5 Large Eggs, Room Temperature (Cage Free)
3/4 Cup Pure Cane Orange Soda
2 Tablespoons Blood Orange or Navel Orange Juice, Freshly Squeezed
1 Teaspoon Pure Orange Extract

Icing

2 1/2 Cups Powdered Sugar
1 Tablespoon Milk (Hemp, Unsweetened Almond Milk or Regular Milk)
1 Tablespoon Pure Orange Flavor
1 Tablespoon Blood Orange Soda
2 Tablespoons Butter, Melted

Recipe Continued On Next Page

Desserts

Preparation: Preheat the oven to 350 degrees. Grease and flour a tube, bundt or large round deep cake pan. In a medium bowl, mix all the dry ingredients together, set aside. In a large bowl, combine sugar and butter until light and creamy; add one at a time until well incorporated; add flavors. Add flour alternately with soda, beginning and ending with flour mixture. Pour cake batter into a prepared pan. Place cake in the center of the oven, and bake for 60-75 minutes or until a toothpick comes out clean. While cake is baking, you can prepare the icing. In a medium bowl, mix all the ingredients together until combined, and pour over slightly warm cake. *Cut cake and serve.*

I wasn't just influenced by my grandmother, father, and countless home cooks and chefs, I was also inspired by a young man I met at Fellowship Missionary Baptist Church where my family attended church. The Pastor, Reverend Clay Evans, introduced Morris Hayes as one of the new musicians at the church. I thought to myself, what can he do that will bring a different spin to the atmosphere of Christian music? Needless to say, that question was answered very quickly. The way Morris played the piano and keyboard touched my soul in ways I didn't think possible. Listening to Morris was quite a beautiful experience. To see him use his God given talent and gift to bless those around him, while also learning from other talented musicians and music directors to develop his craft, was nothing short of amazing. I heard passion every time he played, and I do my best to put forth the same level of passion for my baking, while keeping the tutelage I received from my grandmother and dad at the forefront of my mind.

" Honor her for all that her hands have done, and let her works bring her praise at the city gate." - Proverbs 31:31

Morris used his hands to create glorious music and I use my hands to make delicious cakes. Morris told me once, "As long as you're doing what you're passionate about, you won't have to worry about money. Work hard and go above and beyond what everyone is doing, and you'll succeed."

" Let the favor of the Lord our God be upon us, and establish the work of our hands upon us; yes, establish the work of our hands ." - Psalm 90:17

A mentor doesn't always have to be someone in your field of study, it can be someone God places along your path to show you that by using your hands, you can create something beautiful for God's glory. Morris is a musical genius, mentor, and inspiration; and he has been a source of encouragement during my journey to becoming a better person, baker, and an author.

Desserts

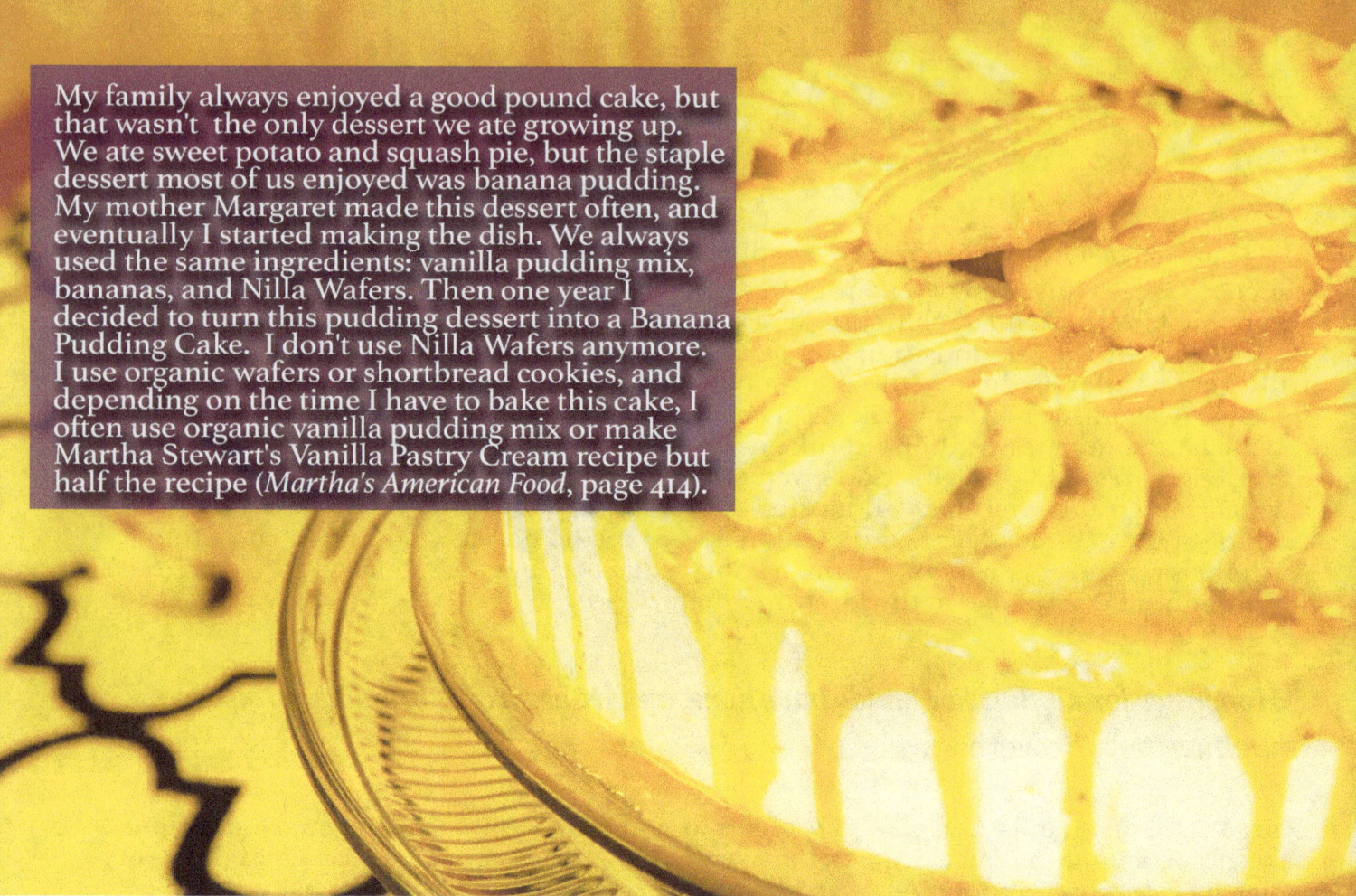

My family always enjoyed a good pound cake, but that wasn't the only dessert we ate growing up. We ate sweet potato and squash pie, but the staple dessert most of us enjoyed was banana pudding. My mother Margaret made this dessert often, and eventually I started making the dish. We always used the same ingredients: vanilla pudding mix, bananas, and Nilla Wafers. Then one year I decided to turn this pudding dessert into a Banana Pudding Cake. I don't use Nilla Wafers anymore. I use organic wafers or shortbread cookies, and depending on the time I have to bake this cake, I often use organic vanilla pudding mix or make Martha Stewart's Vanilla Pastry Cream recipe but half the recipe (*Martha's American Food*, page 414).

Banana Pudding Cake
Serves 10 to 12

Banana Cake

3 Cups All-Purpose Flour, Sifted

1 1/2 Cups Organic or Pure Cane Sugar

1 Teapoon Baking Soda

3 Large Organic Cage Free Eggs, Room Temperature

1/2 Cup Coconut or Canola Oil

2 Teaspoons Pure Vanilla Extract

1 Cup Buttermilk

3 Very Ripe Bananas, Mashed (1 1/2 Cups)

1 Teaspoon Fresh Lemon Juice (For bananas to keep from browning)

3.5 Ounce Vanilla Pudding & Pie Filling (European Gourmet Bakery), or Homemade Vanilla Custard for Filling

Vanilla Wafers (All Natural or Organic) or Shortbread (I used Back to Nature or 365 Organics)

Recipe Continued On Next Page

Preparation: Preheat the oven to 350 degrees. Using a stand mixer combine all the ingredients until just blended. Pour an even amount of cake batter in each of the prepared pans (2-9 inch round). Bake for 35-40 minutes or until the toothpick comes out clean. Remove cakes from oven and let it sit in the pan for 5 to 8 minutes. Turn cake over onto a wire rack to cool completely (about 2 hours).

Buttermilk Frosting

4 1/2 Cups Powdered Sugar
1/2 Stick Unsalted Butter, Softened
1/4 to 1/3 Cup Buttermilk
1 Teaspoon Pure Vanilla Extract
Vanilla Wafers or Shortbread Cookies (a gluten-free version works too)
2 Bananas (thinly sliced) or Banana Chips for Decoration

You can also use French Style or Swiss Meringue Buttercream Frosting (The Cake Book, pages 322-325)

The Organic Vanilla Pudding and Pie Filling mix can be purchased at your nearest Whole Food Market or Online.

In a medium bowl, add softened butter and mix until light; add vanilla. Gradually add powdered sugar with buttermilk until mixed thoroughly and smooth.

Assemble Cake: Place cooled bottom layer on cake or serving plate. Generously brush cake with syrup (optional). Spoon a generous amount of frosting, leaving an open space for the filling. Place bananas on top of filling onto cake. Leave 1/2 inch border around the edge of the cake. Top with last layer, and brush it with more syrup. Frost the sides and top cake with buttermilk frosting. Garnish top of cake with vanilla wafers and sliced banana. Drizzle cake with caramel sauce. Refrigerate cake to set. *Cut and serve.*

Simple Syrup: (Optional)

1/2 Cup Water
1/2 Cup Pure Cane Sugar
1 Teaspoon Vanilla Extract

Preparation: In a small pan, combine water and sugar on medium heat, and cook until sugar dissolves. Continue cooking without stirring until it starts to boil and thicken. Reduce heat to a simmer for five minutes. Remove from heat and stir in vanilla extract. Let syrup cool to room temperature before brushing cake layers.

I've heard that carrots are good for the eyes and they provide multiple vitamins: B1, B2, C, D, and E. Carrots are also rich in potassium, magnesium, folic acid, and calcium, but when I think of carrots, I'm thinking of cake, carrot cake, and not necessarily the healthy aspects of a carrot.

" Let your food be your medicine, and your medicine be your food."- Hippocrates

One day after having lunch with my son, Myles, we decided to grab dessert at The Slice Pizzeria in Rancho Mirage, California. Yep! Myles and I decided on carrot cake. The slice was enormous and absolutely delicious! After the shared slice of cake was eaten, Myles suggested I make a carrot cake that didn't have carrot chunks or shreds. Don't get me wrong, Myles enjoyed the cake, but he has issues with certain textures in food and wanted the carrot cake to be soft and light with the sweetness of carrots in cake form with cream cheese frosting.

A few weeks later as I was creating this cake for Myles, I figured I would steam some carrots, but that seemed like too much work, so I purchased organic carrot baby food (a wonderful shortcut). Shortcuts are allowed. With a few tries, *My Sweet Baby's Carrot Cake* was made. Instead of using the traditional cream cheese frosting that pairs well with carrot cake, I came up with Spiced Buttermilk Frosting. Needless to say, Myles was elated when he took the first bite. I asked him how the cake was, and he put up one finger to silence me, letting me know he was enjoying the carrot cake experience.

" Vegetables are a must on a diet. I suggest carrot cake, zucchini bread, and pumpkin pie." - Jim Davis

Desserts

My Sweet Baby's Carrot Cake

Serves 10 to 12

Spiced Cream Cheese Frosting

1 -4 Ounce Organic or Regular Cream Cheese
1/2 Cup Softened Unsalted Butter
1 Teaspoon Pure Vanilla Extract
4 Cups Powdered Sugar
1/2 Teaspoon Ground Cinnamon
1/4 Teaspoon Ground Nutmeg
Pinch of Sea Salt

Spiced Buttermilk Frosting

1/2 Cup Softened Unsalted Butter
1/2 Teaspoon Ground Cinnamon
1/4 Teaspoon Ground Nutmeg
1 Teaspoon Pure Vanilla Extract
Pinch of Sea Salt
4 Cups Powdered Sugar
3 Tablespoons Buttermilk

Recipe Continued On Next Page

Preparation: In a large bowl, combine cream cheese, butter, and vanilla until creamy. Gradually add powdered sugar until well incorporated. Set aside in a cool place or refrigerate until cake is done and completely cooled. Remove the cake from the refrigerator. Bring frosting to room temperature for spreading consistency before frosting cake.

Carrot Cake:

2 1/4 Cups Unbleached All-Purpose Flour, Sifted
1 Cup Organic Pure Cane Sugar
3/4 Cups Dark or Golden Brown Sugar
3 Large Eggs, Slightly Beaten (Cage Free)
1 Teaspoon Baking Powder
1 Teaspoon Baking Soda
1/2 Teaspoon Fine Sea Salt
1/2 Teaspoon Ground Nutmeg
1 3/4 Teaspoons Ground Cinnamon
1 Cup Pecan Chips
1/2 Cup Unsalted Butter,, Room Temperature
1/2 Cup Canola Oil
2 Teaspoons Pure Vanilla Extract
1/2 Cup Buttermilk
3/4 Cup Pureed Carrots (I used two-4 ounce jars of O Organic Baby Food)
1/2 Cup Raisins (Optional)

Preparation: Preheat the oven to 325 degrees. Grease and flour two 9 inch round or square cake pans. In a medium bowl, combine the dry ingredients, except sugar. In a large bowl, cream the butter and sugars together until light and creamy; add eggs one at a time until mixed thoroughly. Add flour mixture alternately with carrot puree, and buttermilk, beginning and ending with flour, and blend until well combined, being careful not to over mix. Fold in pecans. Pour batter in prepared pans and bake for 35-40 minutes. Insert toothpicks to test for doneness (should come out clean). Cool cake in pans for 5-8 minutes. Let cakes cool completely on a wire rack. Frost top and sides of cake with spice cream cheese or buttermilk frosting and garnish with chopped pecans.

Desserts

One year while visiting my Uncle Ronald and Aunt Lila for a family vacation in Alabama, my aunt said she had something for me and that she knew how much I enjoyed baking. She gave me a recipe for Red Velvet Cake, which was quite popular in the south from what I gathered. It was a humbling experience to say the least, as once again time stood still as she placed the recipe in my hand. My soul stirred! I had never heard of this particular cake until that day, but gladly accepted it and baked it for my family when I returned home. This cake turned out to be one of my mom's favorites, and is another great recipe entrusted to me by a special relative who happens to be a great baker and cook.

"I believe that the soul is the essence of who and what we are. And it comes with codes and possibilities of who we are, who we'll become. It is the lure of our becoming"

- Jean Houston

After years of baking and eating this fabulous red chocolate cake made in its original form, I decided to recreate it. I do not have the original recipe, and I'm going by memory but it included; yellow cake mix, regular red food coloring, baking soda, vinegar, cocoa powder, eggs, and frosted with cream cheese frosting with sprinkled pecans on the top and sides of the cake. Sounds good doesn't it? Who wouldn't enjoy all that deliciousness? It's one of my son's favorite cakes too; and is one of the reasons I decided to recreate this beautiful dessert. I changed the ingredients due to certain allergies and dietary restrictions and modifications. I found that we can still treat ourselves to this classic dessert without feeling guilt or worry, and experience joy with every bite.

"A joyful heart is good medicine, but a crushed spirit dries up the bones."

- Proverbs 17:22

Sticking with the integrity of this cake without losing its delicate texture, I used a red plant-based food color and beet powder for the rich red color and spice undertones. On occasion, I still use cream cheese frosting, but have since switched to sour cream frosting or a traditional buttercream. It is my hope that you enjoy this family favorite as much as my mom and Myles, and while you're at it, have a glass of milk or dessert wine depending on your age.

"A man can do nothing better than to eat and drink and find satisfaction in his work. This too, I see, is from the hand of God." - Ecclesiastes 2:24

Red Velvet Cake
Serves 10 to 12

Sour Cream Frosting

1/4 Cup Unsalted Butter, Softened
1/2 Cup Sour Cream
3 1/2 to 4 Cups Powdered Sugar, Sifted
1 Teaspoon Pure Vanilla Extract

Preparation: In a large bowl of an electric mixer, cream butter at medium speed until creamy. Add sour cream on medium speed until blended and smooth. Gradually add powdered sugar to bowl until incorporated, and light and creamy. Stir in vanilla extract. Set in cool place or refrigerate until cake is ready to frost.

Recipe Continued On Next Page

Cake

2 1/4 Cups Unbleached All-Purpose Flour, Sifted
1 3/4 Cups Organic Pure Cane Sugar
2 Sticks Organic Unsalted Butter, Room Temperature
3 Large Eggs, Cage Free, Room Temperature
1 1/2 Teaspoons Baking Soda, Sifted
1/2 Teaspoon Sea Salt
3 Teaspoons Red Beet Powder, Sifted
2 Tablespoons Pure All-Natural Unsweetened Cocoa or Carob Powder, Sifted
1 Teaspoon Apple Cider Vinegar or Distilled Vinegar
1 1/2 Teaspoons Pure Vanilla Extract
2-3 Bottles of .75 ounce Organic Red Food Color
1 Cup Buttermilk
Bakers Joy Baking Spray with Flour

Preparation: Preheat the oven to 350 degrees. Grease and flour or spray two 9 inch round baking pans. In a large bowl, cream butter and sugar until light and fluffy; add eggs one at a time until incorporated. Mix in vanilla extract. In a medium bowl, sift all dry ingredients. Beginning and ending with flour mixture, add to egg and butter mixture alternately with buttermilk; lastly, mixing in vinegar and red food color. Mix cake batter until well blended, being careful not to over mix. Pour batter into prepared pans and bake 30-35 minutes (darker pans), 35-40 minutes (lighter pans) or until cake tester comes out clean. Let cakes cool in pans for 5-8 minutes. While cake is baking, prepare sour cream frosting. Cool cakes completely on baking racks.

Assemble Cake: Place one of the cooled cake layers upside down on a cake plate or round cake board. Using a small offset spatula, spread 1 cup of sour cream frosting over the top of the layer. Top with the other cake layer, upside down (if the cake comes with a dome top, use a serrated knife to trim excess cake, and reserve extra cake for a snack). Use the rest of the sour cream frosting to frost top and sides of cake. *Garnish cake with chocolate curls.*

Lemon-Lime Ginger Cheesecake Parfaits

Serves 4 to 6

I wanted to challenge myself yet again by entering another recipe contest, and I didn't want to make another cake or cookies, so I created Lime-Ginger Cheesecake. I opted to switch it up for my cookbook, and turn the cheesecake into *Lemon-Lime Ginger Cheesecake Parfaits*. Sometimes you have to change from the mundane to the marvelous, and add just enough citrus to tickle the tastebuds.

Cheesecake Parfaits

2- 8 ounces Cream Cheese, Softened at Room Temperature
2- 5.3 ounces Greek Lime Yogurt
4 Tablespoons Pure Cane Sugar
1/2 Cup Plus 1 Tablespoon Lemon Curd or Fruit Filling (I used Private Selection)
1 1/8 Cup Lime Juice, Fresh Squeezed

Preparation: In a large bowl, combine all the ingredients until smooth and creamy. If by chance the cheesecake mixture is too thick, add a little lime juice to your desired consistency.

Ginger Cookies

1/2 Cup Ginger Cookie, Crushed
2 Tablespoons Pure Cane Sugar
1/2 Teaspoon Ground Cinnamon (Optional)

To Assemble the Parfaits: Using a spoon or piping bag, layer crushed cookies in the bottom of decorative or dessert glasses, then cheesecake filling, cookies, and repeat. Finally, finish the parfaits with a sprinkle of crushed cookies, a lime slice on the rim of glasses, and refrigerate for an hour. *Serve dessert cold.*

Desserts

If it has apples and looks similar to a pie, then it must be a cobbler, the cousin of the apple pie! I'm a huge fan of apple cobbler, but an old neighbor in Chicago asked me if I wanted a recipe for pear cobbler, and I kindly accepted it with open hands. The thing is, I had never made cobbler with pears, but she said I could use canned or fresh pears in this recipe, so I was a happy soul. I've tried the recipe with both, and both ways came out delicious. I've since changed it up a bit. I hope you like it. I've used apples, cherries, blueberries or a combination of two of these fruits for this cobbler. Serve this cobbler with vanilla bean ice cream and caramel sauce. Yummy!

Pear Cobbler

Crust

2- 9 inch Ready Pie Crust/Shells *(or I make the crust from trusted pastry chefs: Michele Albana Stuart-The Pie Lady, or Martha Stewart- Martha's American Food)*

6 Tablespoons Unsalted Butter, Room Temperature

1/4 Cup Organic or All-Natural Pure Cane Sugar

2/3 Cups Unbleached All-Purpose Flour

1 1/8 Teaspoon Sea Salt

Cinnamon (Optional) (I add it because my son loves cinnamon)

Preparation: Preheat the oven to 375 degrees. Beat butter and sugar in a large bowl at medium speed until creamy. Add flour, salt, and cinnamon; mix on low speed until blended. Spread mixture evenly onto bottom of lightly greased 8-inch square pan or 9x13, doubled. Bake crust 15-20 minutes or until crust is light brown. *Only do this step if you want a crust on the bottom of the pear cobbler.

Pear Cobbler/Syrup

1/2 Cup Golden Brown Sugar

1/2 Cup Organic or All-Natural Pure Cane Sugar

3-15 Ounce Cans of Pears or 1 Large Can

1/2 Teaspoon Ground Cinnamon

1/2 Teaspoon Ground Nutmeg

1/2 of Fresh Squeezed Lemon

1/2 Teaspoon Pure Vanilla Extract

2 Teaspoons Corn or Tapioca Starch

2 Teaspoons Water

Recipe Continued On Next Page

Desserts

Orange almond cake

2 Oranges
9 eggs
250g castor sugar
2 teaspoon baking powder
650g ground almonds

Boil oranges in water until soft. Cool and mix to pulp in processor.
Whisk eggs and sugar until thick and creamy.
Fold in baking powder and almonds, then oranges.

Pour into 27cm tin.
Bake 180c for 1 hour.
Glaze cake refer; to orange and lemon cake next page.

Orange and lemon cake

6 eggs
200g sugar
300g ground almonds
1 teaspoon baking powder
1 orange 2 lemons boiled whole for 45 minutes and pureed
100ml grand Marnier

Beat the eggs until light and creamy; add sugar, almonds and baking powder.
Continue beating until soft peaks form. Add the pureed citrus, when well mixed add the liqueur
Pour into lined tin bake 180c for 1 hour.
Remove from oven cool for 20 mins before turning out.

Glaze cake.
Glaze; In a saucepan melt, 200g marmalade with 100ml of grand Marnier simmer stirring from time to time for 3 mins.
Pour over cake.

Serve with cream or crème fraiche.
Will keep in fridge for a week.

Semolina cake

Syrup:
1 ½ cups sugar
 2 cups water
2 Tablespoons orange flower water

Bring to boil and simmer until thin syrup, set aside.

3 eggs
1 ½ cups sugar
Beat until thick and pale add

200g Greek yoghurt
Beat until combined. Add

1 cup semolina
½ cup flour
½ teaspoon baking soda
2 teaspoons baking powder
½ cup ground almonds
160mls vegetable oil
2 teaspoons grated orange rind
Whisk until smooth

Bake in lamington tin 25 – 30 minutes 180 c
Pour syrup over hot cake.

Serve with Greek yoghurt and chopped pistachios.

Rhubarb cake

1 cup sour cream
80g butter
250 g brown sugar
1 teaspoon vanilla essence
grated rind orange
2 large eggs
2 ½ cups flour
1 teaspoon cinnamon
1 teaspoon baking soda
pinch salt
500 g rhubarb chopped uncooked

Cream butter and sugar, then beat in vanilla and grated rind.
Add eggs one at a time beating well.
Add sifted flour cinnamon baking soda and salt alternately with sour cream,
stir in rhubarb last. Mix ½ cup brown sugar and 1 teaspoon cinnamon and sprinkle on top

Bake 180c for 1 hour

Wedding Cake

Moist Chocolate Genoese for wedding cakes

Chocolate 227 g
Boiling water 236g
8 eggs 400g without shells
Castor sugar 200g
Flour plain 150g

Syrup
Castor sugar 88g
Water 182g
Liqueur of choice 40g
Bring to a simmer until sugar has dissolved.

Oven Temperature 180c

In a heavy saucepan bring chocolate and water to boil over low heat, stirring constantly. Simmer 5 mins or until chocolate thickens to a blancmange consistency (It will fall from the spoon and pool slightly before disappearing) Cool completely.

In a large bowl beat eggs and sugar with the whisk beater on high speed for 5 mins or until tripled in volume.
Sift half the flour over the egg mixture and fold in gently but rapidly with a slotted skimmer or large spatula until the flour has disappeared. Repeat with remaining flour until all the flour has disappeared.
Fold in chocolate mixture until incorporated.

Pour immediately into cake tin about 2/3 full and bake 30 mins to 35 mins or until a tester skewer inserted in the centre enters as easily as it does on the sides. And cake pulls slightly away from the sides.
The cake rises to the top and drops slightly.
Sprinkle with the syrup that has been heated with lid on allow to cool before pouring on cake.
Make each layer tin and slice into 3 filled layers to each cake be generous with the pouring syrup.
Ganache each layer, and ganache on the outside to allow the white chocolate icing to adhere to.

Ganache filling
Chocolate 227g
Cream 464 g

Pointers for success
The temperature of the mixture is critical when beating. If not cold it will stiffen, if too cold it will not aerate well. Over beating causes curdling.
Process chocolate in processor, until very fine. Heat cream to boiling point, and with the motor running pour in the cream in a steady stream. Process for a few seconds, until smooth.
Transfer to a large bowl and refrigerate until cold, stirring once or twice about, 2 hours.
Add vanilla essence and beat the mixture until soft peaks form when the beater is raised. It will continue to thicken after a few minutes at room temperature.
If the mixture gets over beaten and grainy it can be restored by re melting chilling and re beating.

Crème Ivoire Deluxe White chocolate icing
White chocolate 680 g
Cocoa butter melted 64g
Clarified butter unsalted 50g
Flavorless oil such as mineral or safflower 50g
Corn syrup 50g
Clarified butter the solids must begin to brown to ensure that all the water in the butter has evaporated. Be sure not a drop of water gets into the melted chocolate.
Put into double boiler chocolate, oil, cocoa butter, corn syrup and clarified butter until melted.

Truffles

Mint Truffles

Large bunch of mint bruised
250 ml cream
Honey a generous pour
Heat to just boil, add
130 grams butter
Block of chocolate

Mix, chill then form into truffles, dip into cocoa powder, or coconut.

Fruit and nut balls (1)

2 cups puffed rice or millet
1 cup of LSA
1½ cups chopped nuts (I use Brazil, raw cashew and macadamia)
1 cup sultanas
1 cup chopped dry fruit (I use dates, but you can use apricots, apple, cranberries or whatever you prefer)
1 cup desiccated coconut (plus extra for rolling the balls in)
½ cup sesame seeds
½ cup sunflower seeds
½ cup pumpkin seeds
1 cup tahini
1 cup honey (may need more to combine the ingredients)

Method Place all ingredients into a large bowl and mix together. Roll into bite size balls and roll in coconut.
This recipe makes a large number of Fruit and nut balls so you can freeze the additional balls.

Fruit and nut balls (2)

1 cup cashews
1 cup almonds
½ teaspoon salt
½ teaspoon cinnamon
½ cup peanut butter
¼ cup coconut oil
1 cup dates
1 teaspoon vanilla essence
100g dark chocolate (optional)

Soak dates in hot water for about half an hour to soften, squeeze out liquid. Pulse cashews and almonds until fine or coarsely ground, add cinnamon salt, peanut butter coconut oil and dates, and pulse until mixed.
To this mixture I mix by hand chopped crystalized ginger, pumpkin seeds, sunflower seeds, dried cranberries, dark chocolate chopped into chunks, fruit and nut mix, trail mix or any mixtures of fruit and nuts you like.
Form into balls and roll into coconut.

I freeze these Fruit and nut balls and then enjoy eating them frozen they soften quite quickly.

Pastry

Hot water pastry

700 g flour
½ teaspoon salt
6 tablespoons milk
150 g lard
2 tablespoons water

Combine flour and salt in a bowl.
Warm the milk and water with the lard, until the lard has melted.
Slowly pour milk into flour and mix.

Knead until smooth, rest for 30 minutes.
This pastry is used for the shell of the pie bottoms.

Short pastry

625gms butter softened
275g sugar
1 egg
50gms milk
Pinch baking powder
1kg flour

Cream butter and sugar add milk and egg then dry ingredients.
Turn out onto lightly floured surface and knead slightly.

This size batch of short pastry is excellent for the slice recipes.
Pastry stores well in fridge wrap in cling wrap.
I also have frozen this raw pastry and when required just bring it to room temperature and re-mold.

Yummy quick pastry

250g flour
60g caster sugar
Pinch salt
180g butter
2 egg yolks
Few drops water

In food processor, combine the flour, sugar and salt and butter and process until bread crumbs.
Add egg yolks and water.
Knead and cover.
Refrigerate 1 hour.

Puff Pastry

250g plain flour
1 teaspoon salt
250g butter
100ml chilled water

Process flour salt and butter to coarsely combined; gradually add water, pulsing until mixture just comes together.
Divide in half and wrap in plastic wrap and refrigerate until firm.
Roll out dough portion on a lightly floured surface until 2 cm thick repeat the same on the other portion, place one layer on top of the other.
Fold one third into the centre, then fold remaining third into the centre, so you have three layers.
Roll out to pie shape and place on top of pie.

Crumpets

375 ml milk
1 teaspoon sugar
2 teaspoons yeast
450 g flour
1 ½ cups tepid water
½ teaspoon salt
1 teaspoon baking soda

Warm milk until tepid add in the sugar and yeast, set aside to activate.
In bowl add flour, pour in yeast mixture, using a whisk or processor, beat until smooth.
Cover with cling film and leave to prove for 1 – 2 hours until batter has doubled.
Whisk in salt and baking soda.

Do a test run first to get right heat and consistency; you may need to add more warm water to get a pour able batter.
Using rings oil rings and pan. Pour in about 2 3 tablespoons of mixture.
Cook on one side for about 5 to 6 minutes, until caramel and large bubbles on top.
Turnover and cook for a few minutes.

Quinoa quiche crust

2 cups cooked quinoa
1 egg white
⅓cup grated parmesan

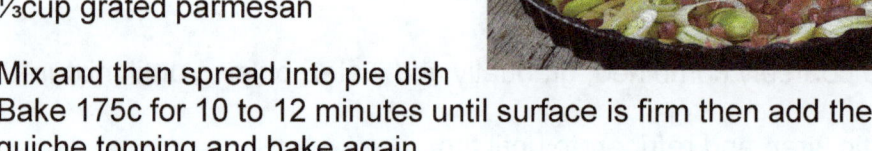

Mix and then spread into pie dish
Bake 175c for 10 to 12 minutes until surface is firm then add the quiche topping and bake again.

Quiche pastry

300gms softened butter
6 cups flour level.
Mix to breadcrumb consistency add in

3 Eggs
1 cup cold water
And Mix

I divide this into about six portions and freeze, return to room temperature
and remold and roll out to about 2mm thick, place into quiche dish, then add in your filling.

Quiche fillings

Grate cheese and spread over quiche pie bottom then add in filling.
Broccoli and cauliflower chopped into chunks and spread over the cheese to fill pie dish. Fill with filling.
Tomato, onion and salami or bacon. Fill with filling.
Asparagus or mushrooms. Fill with filling.
Bake at 175c for about 45 minutes or until when you wobble the dish the centre does not move.
Bring out and cool for about 15 minutes so the filling settles and is easy to cut.
Left over pieces microwaves well.

Filling
5 eggs
400ml milk
200ml cream (is optional but it does make a rich creamy quiche, or replace with milk)
½ teaspoon seasoning

Put ingredients into a bowl and whisk with a fork and pour into quiche dish.

Seasoning ratio; 6 teaspoons salt to 1 teaspoon white pepper, this is the basis to meat pie mixture fillings used in bakeries.

Wonton wrappers

This dough can be made in several ways.

Dough 1
75ml vegetable oil
1¼ cups plain flour
1 tablespoon sugar
3½ tablespoons water

Dough 2
¾ cup plain flour
¼ cup vegetable oil

Knead all ingredients to form a dough leave to rest for 30 minutes.

Dumpling wrappers

3 cups plain flour
1 cup boiling water
3 tablespoons cold water

Place flour in mixer with dough hook slowly add in boiling water and then add cold water.

Steam buns

¼ cup water
5 tablespoons milk
2 ¼ cups flour
½ cup sugar
3 ¼ teaspoons baking powder
2 tablespoons vegetable shortening melted
1 teaspoon white vinegar

Knead altogether until dough is smooth and elastic rest 1 hour
Steam for about 12 to 14 minutes.

Icings - Fillings

Caramel

(1)
350g butter melted
125g golden syrup
650g icing sugar
Melt butter add in golden syrup stirring to stop golden syrup burning to pot bottom slightly caramelize add in icing sugar and stir in fast, spread onto cake base.

(2)
125gms butter
4 tablespoons golden syrup
1.5 tins condensed milk
Heat gently, stirring continuously to stop golden syrup burning to the pot bottom slightly caramelize for about 2 minutes.

(3)
150gms butter
150gms sugar
150gms golden syrup (2 big tablespoons)
2 tins condensed milk (10oz)
Same procedure as above.

Plain icing

125g melted butter
1.5k icing sugar
175ml milk

Mix altogether and add more milk or icing sugar depending on consistency. Consistency should be able to scoop out icing and spatula over slice.

Chocolate icing

125g melted butter
1.5k icing sugar
2 heaped tablespoons cocoa
200ml milk

Mix altogether and add more milk or icing sugar depending on consistency. Consistency should be able to scoop out icing and spatula over slice.

Cream cheese icing

(1)
275g cream cheese
1.225kg icing sugar
75g water

(2)
1kg cream cheese
3 cups icing sugar
3teaspoonsvanilla essence
150g cup melted butter

Choose the recipe and put into blender and blend or mix with a beater.

Slices

Tan squares

700g melted butter
450g sugar
1.250g flour
2 teaspoons vanilla

Mix altogether then press ¾ of the mixture into a slice tin.
Bake 175c for about 15 minutes take out of oven and then pour over the caramel.
Crumble the rest of mixture on top.
Bake until lightly golden on top

Caramel.
2 tin condensed milk
4 tablespoon golden syrup
250g butter melted
Put all ingredients into a pot, heat over gentle heat and stir to avoid burning to pot bottom

Sultana squares or Apple slice

Short pastry, in (pastry section)
Roll out and place into slice tin, prick randomly over the pastry this will prevent the pastry from shrinking while baking.
Bake 170c for about 15 minutes, just enough to set the pastry, because it will be further baked for the top.
The pre-bake is to stop the pastry from being under baked.

Sultana mix; Mix sultanas with lemon peel and cake crumbs, a little sugar and water. If no cake crumbs use bread crumbs.

Apple mix; Stewed apples with some sugar for sweetness, then drain of the liquid, to this you can add cinnamon or even sultanas. Place the mixture you want over the base working quickly then.
Place another layer of pastry on top.
Prick with a fork and glaze with egg white and sprinkle sugar on top.
Bake 170c for about 20 minutes.

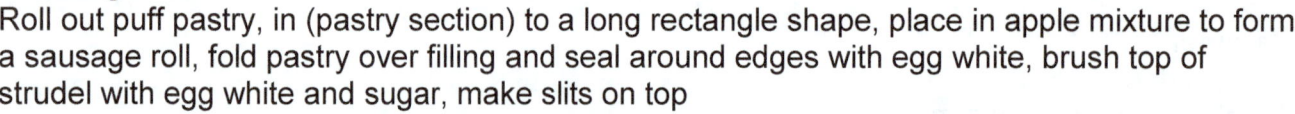

Apple strudel

2 tins stewed apple or home stewed apples

1 cup sultanas
1 cup currants
100gms sugar

3 teaspoons mixed spice
2 teaspoons cinnamon

Mix altogether.
Roll out puff pastry, in (pastry section) to a long rectangle shape, place in apple mixture to form a sausage roll, fold pastry over filling and seal around edges with egg white, brush top of strudel with egg white and sugar, make slits on top

Bake 180c for about 20 to 30 minutes.

Jumble

250g butter melted
200gms flour
130g brown sugar
125g coconut
1 teaspoon baking powder
25g cocoa
25g kornies or corn flakes

Put all the dry ingredients into a
the butter add to the dry ingredients.
Pour into a slice pan and press down.

Bake 175c about 30minutes

Ice with chocolate icing, in
(icing section) and sprinkle coconut on top.

Fudge

2 tablespoons maltexo or malt
500g butter melted
700g brown sugar
700g condensed milk
Mix then add
250g coconut
80g rice bubbles
450g sultanas
1kilo malt biscuits lightly crushed

Mix all the ingredients together, pour into slice dish and press down.

Ice with chocolate icing in the (icing section), sprinkle with coconut. Best kept in fridge.

Ginger slice

300g butter melted
150g sugar
420g flour
1 teaspoon baking powder
3 teaspoons ginger

Mix altogether press into slice tin
Bake 175c for about 30 minutes. Ice while hot with topping.

Topping
250g butter
250g golden syrup.
750g icing sugar
3tsp ginger

In a larger pot melt the butter and golden syrup stirring to avoid burning the golden syrup, when melted add the icing sugar and ginger and stir until combined, and then pour over hot slice and spread.

Optional; add to garnish on top of slice roughly chopped crystallized ginger, lightly press into icing.

Peanut slice

400g flour
1tsp baking powder
250g sugar
250g coconut
200g raw peanuts
50g cornflakes
350g melted butter
70g golden syrup

Put dry ingredients into a bowl
Melt butter and golden syrup then add to dry ingredients.
Press into slice tray.
Bake 175c for about 30 - 40minutes.
Ice while hot with topping.

Topping
170g butter
1 tablespoons golden syrup
450g icing sugar
Melt butter add golden syrup while on heat add icing sugar stirring until smooth.
Pour over hot slice.

Optional add to topping roasted peanuts.
In a bowl add the butter condensed milk vanilla essence icing sugar and coconut mix altogether, spread on top of jam. Sprinkle coconut on top.

Churchill square

170g butter
170g sugar
Cream then add
2 eggs
340g flour
1 ½ teaspoon baking powder

Mix altogether; divide the mixture by putting 3/4 of the dough into a bowl, mix in 3 tablespoons cocoa.

Press this into a slice tin; spread raspberry jam over the top.

With the other 1/4 of dough, put in
1 tin condensed milk
1 ½ cups coconut
Mix altogether
Spread this over the jam, the easy way to spread is to put spoonsful of the mixture over the jam and then use the back of the spoon to blend the mixture together.

Bake 175c for 30 minutes.

Ice with chocolate icing, in (icing section) sprinkle with coconut.

Coconut Ice slice

Short pastry, in (pastry section) Roll out and place into slice tin, prick randomly over the pastry this will prevent the pastry from shrinking while baking. Bake 170c for about 20 minutes Spread with raspberry jam

350g butter softened
1 tin condensed milk
Vanilla essence
600g icing sugar
225g coconut
Mix the above ingredients altogether and spread over jam.
Sprinkle desiccated coconut on top.
This slice is best kept in refrigerator.

Rocky road

Short pastry, in (pastry section) Roll out and place into slice tin,
prick randomly over the pastry this will prevent the pastry from shrinking while baking. Bake 170c for about 20 minutes.
Spread with raspberry jam

Topping
250g sugar
250g coconut
100g butter
100ml milk
1 teaspoon vanilla essence
250g sultanas
20 chopped cherries
Mix the above ingredients and pour topping over jam.

Bake 175c for about 30 minutes or until slightly golden on top.

Russian slice

450g flour
2 teaspoons baking powder
350g butter
250g walnuts
350g sugar
250g whole ginger
8eggs
4 tablespoons milk
1 cup currants
Pinch salt

Cream butter and sugar; add eggs one at a time.
Put nuts and ginger into blender and mince.
Mix all the ingredients together with currants.

Bake 175c about 1 hour.
Ice with white icing, in
(icing section),
sprinkle coconut on top.

Peppermint slice

250g butter
250g sugar
2 eggs
360g flour
1 teaspoon baking powder
125g kornies or cornflakes
100g bourn vita or cocoa

Cream butter and sugar add in eggs and beat, then add in flour and baking powder and mix in slowly the cornflakes or kornies.
Spread onto a slice dish.
Bake 175c for about 30 minutes, should be a soft feel when touched.

Make Peppermint icing. Depending on how thick you want the icing just mix hot water, icing sugar and peppermint essence, together. Spread on top of base and leave to chill.
Make a chocolate icing, in (icing section) and spread over the peppermint icing.

Belgium slice

300g butter
140g sugar
1 heaped tablespoon golden syrup
1 egg
10ml milk
500g flour
1 teaspoons cinnamon
1 teaspoon mixed spice
1 teaspoons ginger
½ teaspoons baking powder

Cream butter and sugar add golden syrup egg mix in add in milk and mix then add in dry ingredients and mix.

Divide mixture, roll out and place in slice dish. Spread with raspberry jam (if jam is too stiff to spread, mix in a bowl with a little hot water to a spreadable consistency.
Roll out other portion and place on top of jam.
Bake175c for about 30 – 40 minutes.

Ice with white icing, in (icing section), sprinkle the icing with red jelly crystals or cochineal and sugar mixed together.

To make Belgium biscuits roll out and cut out round cookie shapes, bake for about 15 minutes, leave to cool, spread with jam and join with a second baked cookie, ice with white icing and sprinkle with the red crystals.

Rock melon slice

2 ½ portions weetbix
175 g melted butter
125 g flour
175 g sugar
1 teaspoons baking powder
1 cup coconut
2 tablespoons cocoa

Mix dry ingredients to butter.
Press into slice tin.
Bake 180c for 15 minutes.

Top with marshmallow.

Marshmallow.
Dissolve 2 dessertspoons gelatin in 1 cup boiling water add 2 cups sugar, vanilla and colour beat till fluffy.
Pour overcooled base. Sprinkle with coconut.

Or melt 200 g chocolate with ½ cup water and beat well, gradually beat in 175 g butter in small pieces till smooth. Chill till mixture thickens to slightly pourable consistency and spread over marshmallow.

Coconut crumble

Short pastry, in (pastry section) Roll out and place into slice tin, prick randomly over the pastry this will prevent the pastry from shrinking while baking.
Bake 170c for about 20 minutes.
Spread with raspberry jam

500g sugar
500g coconut
225g butter softened
225g milk
1 teaspoon vanilla

Mix altogether.
Spread over the raspberry jam
Bake 175c until light brown.

Coconut macaroon

Short pastry, in (pastry section) Roll out and place into slice tin, prick randomly over the pastry this will prevent the pastry from shrinking while baking.
Bake 170c for about 15 minutes, just enough to set the pastry, because it will be further baked for the top. The pre-bake is to stop the pastry from being under baked.
Spread over pastry base caramel or lemon honey
Caramel in the filling section

Top with macaroon.

Macaroon
4 egg whites
100g sugar

Beat egg whites till stiff add sugar and beat.
Fold in only
170g coconut
100g sugar

Bake in cool oven 140c for 30 minutes turn off oven and leave in oven to cool.
For a thicker macaroon topping, double the quantity.

Biscuits

Mums biscuits

4 cups flour
350 g butter
350 g sugar

2 teaspoons baking soda
Almond essence or grated lemon rind.

Cream butter and sugar add in dry ingredients and essence and mix.
Lightly flour surface and roll out, shape with cookie cutter or just cut into squares.
Glaze with egg white, put slivered almonds or grated lemon rind and a little sprinkle of sugar on top.

Bake 175c for 12 minutes
Leave on tray for a few minutes to set the biscuit then remove from tray.

Anzac biscuits

250 g flour
300g sugar
2 cups coconut
2 cups rolled oats
1 teaspoon baking soda
200 g butter
2 tablespoons golden syrup

Place dry ingredients into a bowl.
Melt butter and golden syrup in a pot, pour into dry ingredients and mix.
Mold with your hands into balls and press onto baking tray

Bake 175c for 15 minutes
Leave on tray for a few minutes to set the biscuit then remove from tray.

Kiwi biscuits

450gms butter
700 g flour
350 g sugar
4 teaspoons baking powder
4 tablespoons condensed milk
Salt
2 teaspoons vanilla
Chocolate chips.

Cream butter and sugar add dry ingredients and mix.
Place on lightly floured surface and knead then roll into a log about 6 cm in diameter, slice to 10 to 15mm thickness place each portion onto baking tray.

Bake 175c for 10 to 15 minutes
Leave on tray for a few minutes to set the biscuit then remove from tray.

Lolly cake

625g crumbed biscuits
250g butter melted
1 tin condensed milk
225g Eskimos or fruit puffs

Melt butter add ingredients, and mix.
Roll into a log and wrap in glad wrap.
Chill then unwrap cling wrap and slice 15mm portions. Keep stored in fridge.
This cake freezes well.

Mays shortbread

500g butter
350g castor sugar
50g corn flour
½ teaspoon salt
675g flour

Cream butter and sugar add dry ingredients and mix.
Place onto a lightly floured surface, roll out into a log shape,
then slice 15mm size portions, place onto baking tray prick two times with a fork for the pattern.

Bake 160c for 30 minutes.

Deluxe shortbread

780 g softened butter
340 g icing sugar
770 g flour
250 g custard powder
Pinch salt

Cream icing sugar and butter add dry ingredients.
Place onto a lightly floured surface, roll out into a log shape, then slice 15mm size portions, place onto baking tray prick two times with a fork for the pattern.

Bake 160c for 30 minutes

Lavosh Crackers

Oregano 1 tablespoon chopped or dried
1 cup flour
⅓ cup whole meal flour or plain flour
2 Tablespoon sesame seeds
1 teaspoon salt
Black pepper
½ cup water
¼ cup olive oil
1 teaspoon sesame oil

Mix altogether
Roll out thinly, about 1-2mm sprinkle salt over the top and roll salt in.
Roll back onto rolling pin to pick up and place onto baking tray, then cut into lines the sizes you want, I just do random shapes.

Bake 175c for about 15-20 minutes. I like mine dry, so I take of the pieces that look done and keep baking the rest for a minute or two.
This mixture makes about 5 trays.

Keeps well and is so yummy to eat pain, or as a cracker replacement.

Muffins - Breads Scones

Sugar buns

2 cups flour
3 teaspoons baking powder
½ cup sugar
2 tablespoons sultanas
1 egg whisked
75 g melted butter
1 teaspoons vanilla
⅓ cup milk

In a bowl add the flour baking powder sugar and sultanas slightly mix together.
In another bowl mix melted butter, egg, and milk then add to dry ingredients and mix, if dough is not pliable add a little more milk.
Make into bun portions, sprinkle sugar on top.

Bake 200c for 10 minutes
Cut in half and spread with butter.

Scones

3 cups self-rising flour
Pinch salt
150g grated butter
1¼ cups milk

Lightly mix the ingredients by hand.
Press out to about 4cm thick and cut to the sizes you want.
The trick to a good scone is not to over mix the dough, and the grated butter greatly improves the texture.

Bake 230c for 10-15 minutes

This dough can be made into savoury scones by pressing out to about 2cms thick and line half the scone with a chutney, grated cheese, chopped onions, herbs, chopped bacon or salami, and or chopped sun dried tomatoes, Fold over and press down to seal, make cuts to the sizes you want.
Or roll into a pin wheel log and slice 4 cm portions and lay out flat on baking tray to bake.

Muffins

3 cups flour
1 cup sugar
4 teaspoons baking powder
Pinch salt
Place the above ingredients into a large bowl and mix with wooden spoon.

Whisk together
2 eggs
1 cup milk
150 ml melted butter
Add this to the dry ingredients, fold, and do not over mix or you will create a tough muffin. This is the base ingredients, to add variations of muffins add fruit or chocolate and spices to the dry ingredients.

Variations:
2 teaspoons ground ginger and crystalized chopped ginger and chopped pears.
White chocolate chunks and strawberries.
Edible Lavender flowers and white chocolate chunks.
Mixed berries and 1 teaspoon mixed spice.
1 tablespoon cocoa and dark chocolate chunks.
Grated apple and 1 teaspoon cinnamon.

Bake 190c for 20 minutes or until skewer comes out clean, leave in muffin tray for a few minutes and they should come out clean.

Coconut bread

2 eggs
300 ml milk
1 teaspoon vanilla
2 ½ cups flour
2 teaspoon baking powder
2 teaspoons cinnamon
1 cup caster sugar
150 g coconut
75 g melted butter

Lightly whisk egg and liquid.
Add to dry ingredients. Add melted butter and stir until mixture is smooth, don't over mix.

Bake 180 c for 1 hour. Cool in tins 5 mins.

Batter can be put into fridge for 2 days before baking.

Toast and serve with lime marmalade, or just with butter.

Olliebollen Donuts (Dutch doughnut)

1 teaspoon yeast
1 cup lukewarm milk
2 ¼ cups plain flour
1 teaspoon sugar
2 teaspoons salt
1 egg
¾ cup dried currants
¾ cup raisins
1 granny smith apple peeled and grated
Icing sugar for dusting
Oil for frying

Pour yeast over warm milk with the sugar. Let stand for a few minutes.
Place flour in bowl with the egg and salt mix into a smooth batter. Stir in the dried fruits and grated apple.
Cover bowl and leave in a warm place to rise, will take about 1 hour.
Heat the oil in a deep fryer to 190c.
Use two metal spoons to shape and scoop dough balls and drop carefully into oil.
Fry balls until golden brown turn them over about 8 minutes.
The doughnuts should be soft and not greasy.
If the oil is not hot enough the outside will be tough and the inside greasy.
Drain cooked doughnuts on paper towels and dust with icing sugar.
Serve on a platter with more icing sugar, best eaten hot.

Pikelet batter

3 eggs
2 ½ cups milk
1teasppon vanilla essence
110 ml melted butter
1 ½ tablespoons sugar
1 ½ heaped tablespoons baking powder
3 cups flour

Put all ingredients into food processor and whiz until the batter is smooth. Place spoonsful onto hot pan,
turn over and cook the other side when bubbles start to form.

Christmas Cakes

Christmas cake

700 g butter
700 g brown sugar
3 tablespoons treacle
12 eggs
250 ml cold black tea
125 ml brandy
2 teaspoon vanilla essence
700 g flour
2 teaspoon baking powder
1 teaspoon salt
3 teaspoon mixed spice
1 teaspoons cinnamon
1 teaspoons nutmeg
Grated lemon rind.
2 kg of a mixture of sultanas, currants, cherries, mixed peel, almonds and mixed fruit

Cream the butter and sugar.
Mix the flour, salt baking powder, and spices in a separate bowl.
Beat in another bowl the treacle, eggs, liquid and essence just enough to break up the eggs.
Then add this to the butter sugar mixture, mixing it altogether, it won't combine fully and will look separated, that is okay.

Have a large basin container, add this liquid to this basin, then add the dry ingredients a bit at a time and mix with your hand to combine the ingredients, and then add your mixed fruit.

Line a large cake tin or two medium cake tins with cardboard and then baking paper, the cardboard prevents the cake from drying out on the edges.
Pour batter mixture into tins to about two cm from the top.

Bake in slow oven 130c for about 4 hours for large cakes
2 hours for small cakes.
If it takes longer to bake in a slow oven that is okay, test with a skewer.
Just don't over bake the cake or have the oven too hot, the fruit will burn, and you will just create a bitter burnt cake.

Jewel cake

1kg dried dates
500 g dried pineapple
150 g dried red cherries
150 g dried green cherries
500 g dried papaya chunks
150 g dried ginger
250 g sultanas
Soak the above dried ingredients overnight with rum 150 ml

Then add to this mix, the nuts
125 g whole raw almonds
300 g Brazil nuts
125 g walnuts

6 eggs
300 g brown sugar
3 teaspoons vanilla
3 tablespoons rum
270 g butter softened
Beat eggs until light and fluffy. Add sugar, vanilla, rum, and softened butter. Continue till well blended.

225 g plain flour
2 teaspoon baking powder
1 teaspoon salt
Sift flour with baking powder and salt.
Have a large basin container, add the creamed ingredients to the basin then add the dry ingredients a bit at a time and mix with your hand to combine the ingredients, and then add your mixed fruits and nuts. Mix well

Pour into cake tins lined with baking paper on the bottom.
Bake in slow oven 130c about 2 hours or until firm to touch cake.

When baked, glaze with sugar water mixture.

Bring to boil ½ cup sugar and ½ cup water simmer for a few minutes, (optional add a tablespoon of marmalade then brush the top of the cake. This gives the cake a shine.
Cool in tin.

I used to make and sell this cake throughout New Zealand and I had an excess of stock which was a year old, they were sealed, I was about to throw them all away but before I did I tried one of them, it was the most decadent cake I have ever eaten, I ended up selling all of them at a market with a taste test.

Breads

Gluten Free Bread

1 cup sorghurn flour
2/3 cup amaranth flour
½ cup cornmeal
¼ cup quinoa flour
⅓ cup tapioca flour
⅓ cup brown sugar
1 tablespoon Xntham gum
1 tablespoon bread yeast
1 ½ teaspoon salt
2 eggs
1 egg white
1 cup water
2 tablespoons oil
1 teaspoon cider vinegar

Mix the liquid ingredients together with the eggs.
Add the rest of the mixture.
Beat for about 4 minutes

Pour into loaf tin. Leave to rise covered for about 1 hour
Bake 175c for 35 to 45 minutes until hollow sound.

Spelt biscuits

¾ cups packed brown sugar
½ cup butter, softened
1 egg
1 teaspoon vanilla extract
1 ¾ cups spelt flour, or more if needed
1 teaspoon baking soda
½ teaspoon salt
½ cup chocolate chips (optional)
½ cup chopped pecans (optional)

Cream butter and sugar, add egg and mix in, add essence and dry ingredients.
Place spoonsful on baking tray.

Bake 175C for about 15 minutes.

Spelt bread

Makes 2 big loaves
8 cups spelt flour
½ cup sesame seeds
½ teaspoon salt, or to taste
1 tablespoon blackstrap molasses
2 teaspoons baking soda
4 ¼ cups milk

Preheat the oven to175c Grease two loaf pans.

In a large bowl, mix together the spelt flour, sesame seeds, salt, molasses, baking soda and milk until well blended.
Divide the batter evenly between the prepared pans.
Bake for 1 hour and 10 minutes or until golden.

Placing a tin of the same size over the top of the loaf while baking gives it a lovely crust

Spelt bread 2

Makes 2 big loaves

2 teaspoons active dry yeast
1 tablespoon sugar
7 cups spelt flour
2 cups warm water
1 tablespoon salt

Stir yeast and sugar, gradually adding warm water. Add about half the flour and the salt and beat well. Add the remainder of the flour gradually to acquire stiff dough. It may require more or less than 7 cups of spelt flour.
Knead 5 to 10 minutes until smooth and elastic.
Put dough into a buttered bowl and turn once to butter surface. Cover with a towel and let rise until doubled, keeping it in a warm place to rise about 2 hours.
Punch down dough with your fist and divide into two parts.
Knead and shape into 2 loaves and place into loaf pans. Cover again and allow dough to rise to top of pans.

Bake 175c in two greased loaf tins for 50 minutes

Gluten Free Vegan Bread

This bread has a tender crust and is soft and light on the inside. It doesn't crumble. You can slice it thin and it doesn't fall apart.

3 cups gluten flour mix (GF) (below)
2 teaspoons xanthan gum
½ teaspoon salt
3 tablespoons sugar
1 teaspoon dry yeast
2 teaspoon coconut oil
160ml warm water

Grease and dust with GF flour a 8x4 loaf tins.
Combine GF Flour Mix, xanthan gum, salt, sugar, and dry yeast in a medium sized bowl and whisk together. Set aside.
In mixing bowl, combine the coconut oil and warm water together and then add the dry ingredients. Mix for 2 minutes, it should resemble a thicker cake batter. Pour batter into prepared loaf tins and cover with a tea towel, leave in warm place to rise to nearly the top.

Bake at 200c for 20 minutes and cover with foil loosely to prevent over browning bake for a further 25 minutes.
Test with a skewer, (optional you can rub the top of the loaf with some coconut oil to glaze)
Leave to cool completely before cutting.

Gluten Flour Mix

1 ½ cups millet flour
1 ½ cups sorghum flour
1 cup tapioca flour
1 cup potato starch
1 cup arrowroot powder

Multi-grain bread

1 cup corn starch
1 cup tapioca starch
2/3 cup chickpea/garbanzo bean flour
½ cup sorghum flour
¼ cup millet or quinoa flour
2 teaspoon xanthan gum
1 ½ teaspoon agar powder
1 teaspoon salt

Place the above in a bowl.

¾ cup warm water
1½ tablespoons maple syrup
2 ¼ teaspoon active yeast

Place the above in a bowl to prove.

9 tablespoon cold water,
3 tablespoons ground flaxseeds, soak for 5 minutes. Then add
¾ cup soda water
3 tablespoons olive oil or other oil
¾ teaspoon cider vinegar

Add wet ingredients to dry ingredients and stir to combine, (mixture will be very thick and soft dough).
Cover and let rise for about 1 hour

Bake 200c for 40 to 45 minutes cool in pan for 10 minutes
Variation: add any seeds to the mixture pumpkin, sun flower seeds, chia, and sesame seeds.

Hot Desserts

Sago Plum Pudding

4 tablespoons sago
1¾ cups milk
1 cup fresh breadcrumbs
½ cup raisins
½ cup sultanas
¼ cup mixed peel
20g butter
1 cup sugar
1 teaspoon mixed spice
1 teaspoon baking soda

Soak sago in ¾ of the milk for 2 hours.

Add all ingredients.

Dissolve the soda in the cup of milk and add to mixture.
Pour into greased steamer mold, cover steam bowl with lid.
Fill a large pot with boiling water so it reaches to about 4cm below the steamer bowl lid; simmer in the large pot with lid on for 4 hours, checking periodically to add more water reduced from evaporation.

Sticky date pudding

680g dates
4 teaspoons baking soda
680g sugar
240g butter
8 eggs
680g flour
8 teaspoons baking powder
2 teaspoons vanilla essence

Pour 1.2 litres water over dates and bring to the boil.
Remove from heat and add baking soda, leave to lukewarm.

Cream butter and sugar; add eggs one at a time, beating well.
Fold in flour, stir in date mixture and vanilla essence and pour into a large roasting tin.
Bake 160c for 30-40 minutes

Sauce
800g Brown sugar
2 cups cream
400g butter
2 teaspoons vanilla essence
Bring to the boil, reduce heat and simmer, pour over date cake when baked.

This dessert freezes well. Cut into portions and heat in microwave.
This dessert never stays around long it is just too Moorish.

Apple Crumble

Stewed apples or any fruit, fill pie dish half way with the fruit.
Note; I usually use a casserole dish and place the fruit to about three quarters full, depending on the fruit I sprinkle a little sugar to sweeten then put the casserole lid on, and microwave on high about 6 minutes to soften the fruit, it will cook further when in the oven.

2 cups plain flour
2 teaspoons baking powder
1 cup sugar
250g butter room temperature

Rub the above ingredients together to form a dough crumb or put into a blender and mix.
I like mine to be slightly buttery dough, where the dough can crumble to resemble fine to small marble sizes to go on top, when baked it is crunchy and really very nice.
If mixture is too buttery and like a paste add a little more flour, it must be able to crumble.

Bake 175c for about 30 minutes or until slightly golden on top.

P.S I like to bake the crumb in a baking dish with no fruit, and turning a few times to evenly bake, I like this crumb on ice-cream, plain or with maple syrup.

Individual steamed puddings

6 tablespoons jam, marmalade or jelly
Few teaspoons water or liqueur
Fruit of choice
125g butter chilled
1 cup self-rising flour
1 cup fresh white bread crumbs
½ cup brown sugar
1 egg
2 tablespoons milk

Grease six small ramekins.

Soften the jam add water or liqueur and mix well, spoon into ramekins.
Rub butter and flour, add bread crumbs and sugar.
Beat egg and milk together and mix into dry ingredients, this can be done in a food processor.
Spoon dough evenly into ramekins.

Place ramekins into roasting dish fill with hot water to half way up the ramekins; cover the whole roasting dish with tin foil bake 180c for 45 minutes.
To serve remove puddings from oven and allow standing for 5 minutes, turn upside down to remove pudding from ramekin.

Serve with whipped cream.

Golden winter pudding

150g butter
150g sugar
2 eggs
150g self-rising flour
2 tablespoons milk
3 heaped tablespoons golden syrup

Cream the butter and sugar.
Slowly beat in eggs, fold in flour and milk.
Grease steamer pudding bowl pour the golden syrup into the pudding bowl and then pour batter over the golden syrup.

Additional extra sprinkle 2 tablespoons of shredded coconut onto the golden syrup.
Cover steamer bowl with lid.

Fill a large pot with water and bring to the boil, the steamer should reach to about 4cm below the steamer bowl lid; simmer in the large pot with lid on for 1¼ hours, checking periodically to add more water reduced from evaporation.

Steam Pudding

Grate orange zest
3 bay leaves
6 tablespoons maple syrup
210 grams butter
210 grams sugar
3 teaspoon baking powder
100 grams self-rising flour
1 teaspoon cloves
¼ teaspoon salt

Cream the butter and sugar
Beat eggs add to butter and slowly beat.
Fold in dry ingredients.

Into pudding greased steamer bowl place maple syrup and orange zest with 3 bay leaves in the bottom, top with the mixture.
Cover steamer bowl with lid.
Fill a large pot with boiling water so it reaches to about 4cm below the steamer bowl lid; simmer in the large pot with lid on for 1½ hours, checking periodically to add more water reduced from evaporation.

Christmas Steamed pudding (makes 2 puddings)

250g figs
250g candies peel
225g raisins
225g currants
125g sultanas
125g glace cherries
125g crystallized ginger
125g almonds
1 carrot grated
Finely grated zest 2 oranges
Finely grated zest 1 lemon
75ml beer
75ml brandy
225g butter
225g sugar
4 eggs
50g flour
1 teaspoon mixed spice
½ teaspoon nutmeg
½ teaspoon salt
225g fresh breadcrumbs

Mix all fruit, zest and nuts with brandy and beer.
Cream the butter and sugar, add in eggs one at a time.
Add in flour and spices along with bread crumbs, mix by hand if necessary.
Butter 2 x 4 cup pudding steamer bowls.
Cover steamer bowl with lid.

Fill a large pot with boiling water so it reaches to about 4cm below the steamer bowl lid; simmer in the large pot with lid on for 6 hours, checking periodically to add more water reduced from evaporation.
This mixture can be halved.
Serve with brandy cream or Anglaise vanilla custard.

Anglaise custard and Brandy cream

2 vanilla beans
250ml milk
250ml cream
4 egg yolks
150g sugar

Split vanilla bean and place in with milk and cream, heat over slow heat until just before it starts to boil, take out the vanilla bean pods.
Whisk egg yolks in a bowl with sugar until creamy, whisking at the same time slowly pour in a little of the hot milk about a cup, until blended, pour back into the hot milk pot whisking, and then stir constantly with a wooden spoon until the mixture coats the wooden spoon and is thickened.
Take of heat.

I normally pour the mixture through a sieve to catch any lumps from the eggs.
Cover with cling film resting it on the custard top to avoid a dry lid to form on top of the custard.

Brandy cream; either use all the above custard or a portion of it, and add in some brandy to your acquired taste, whip up some cream and fold altogether.

Frangipane Tart

Sable pastry
200g butter
100g icing sugar
Pinch salt
2 egg yolks
250g flour

This pastry does not like to be over worked.
Rub butter and icing sugar, add in egg yolks and then flour.
Knead lightly.
Allow pastry to rest.

Filling
100g castor sugar
100g butter
25 g flour
2 eggs
100 g lightly roasted and then ground almonds
Dash of kirsch.

Cream butter and sugar and beat until creamy.
Beat eggs and fold into the butter mixture, add the kirsch and almonds.
Line pie tin with sable pastry, prick all over.
Pour in the frangipane mixture.
Place cherries or poached fruit or plain fruit on top of mixture

Bake 190c for 25-30 minutes

Cold Desserts

The ultimate chocolate mousse

3 eggs separated
200g dark chocolate melted
100 ml cream lightly whipped

Stir egg yolks into melted chocolate until well blended. Whisk egg whites until stiff, fold into chocolate mixture until evenly blended.
Fold in whipped cream and spoon into glasses to set.

Chocolate mousse in minutes

100g chocolate
250g mascarpone
2 tablespoons icing sugar
Cognac
Melt chocolate; quickly beat in mascarpone icing sugar and cognac.

Butter scotch whip

300ml cream
300ml custard
Whip cream add custard, fold in toffee sauce.

Caramel Sauce

1 cup cream
2 cups brown sugar
8 tablespoons butter
½ teaspoon vanilla

In a pot bring the brown sugar
butter and cream to a rolling boil.

Lower the heat stirring constantly,
for about two minutes,
take of heat and add in the essence.
Really delicious with ice-cream.

Toffee sauce

Heat 50g butter
50g muscovite sugar
2 tablespoons golden syrup or honey

Bring to boil until sugar has dissolved,

Simmer 2 minutes stir in 2 tablespoons cream.

Crème Brulees

3 cups cream
6 egg yolks
90 g sugar
1 teaspoon vanilla
¾ cup brown sugar

Heat cream until it reaches boiling point.
Beat the egg yolks with the sugar, stir in a little cream into the yolks, and pour mixture back into cream.
Cook custard over low heat until cream coats wooden spoon, take care not to boil, add vanilla, pour through a sieve into molds and refrigerate overnight.
Place sugar on top and grill until caramelized

Meringues with Kaffir lime syrup and fruit

240ml egg white
Beat egg whites until stiff add
440gms icing sugar and beat
Add and fold in
4 ½ tablespoons corn flour
1 ½ teaspoons cream of tarter
1 tablespoon vinegar

Place spoonful's onto baking paper.
A trick is to stop paper folding up place a small dollop of meringue under each corner of the baking paper.

Bake 120C 1 hour and 10 minutes, leave in oven to cool with door open.

Syrup
100gms palm sugar
250mls water
3 kaffir lime leaves
3 slices of fresh ginger
Bring to boil and simmer until syrupy.

Whip cream and place on top of meringues place slices of mango lychees and papaya with very thin kaffir lime leaf slices and drizzle with syrup.

Chocolate truffle cake with raspberry sauce

2 cups cream
3 egg yolks
500g dark chocolate
½ cup corn syrup dark or light
125g butter
¼ cup icing sugar
1 teaspoon vanilla essence

Line a 23 x 12 cm loaf tin with cling film.

Mix ½ cup cream with egg yolks.

In a saucepan over medium heat stir in chocolate, corn syrup and butter until smooth and well combined.
Add egg mixture and stir constantly for a further 3 mins. Cool to room temperature.
Beat remaining cream with icing sugar and vanilla until soft peaks form
Fold into the chocolate mixture.

Pour into plastic lined loaf tin.
Refrigerate overnight.

Carefully lift out of tin unwrap cling film and slice with hot knife.
Serve with raspberry sauce.

Berry sauce
2 cups fresh or frozen berries
¼ cup sugar to taste
In food processor puree berries with sugar, strain and chill.

Suggestions for chocolate truffle.
Chocolate truffle with peppermint choc sauce
Mocha loaf with coffee liqueur sauce
Grand Marnier or Cointreau with choc sauce garnished with orange or mandarin segments.

Baked Cheesecake with sour cream topping

250g flour
60g caster sugar
Pinch salt
180g butter
2 egg yolks
Few drops water

In food processor, combine the flour, sugar and salt; add butter and process until bread crumbs.
Add egg yolks and water. Knead and cover. Refrigerate 1 hour.

Roll pastry and place pastry into 20cm spring tin. Bake for about 15 minutes.

400g cream cheese
2 x 395 g cans condensed milk
4 eggs
450mls cream
1 teaspoon vanilla essence
Juice of lemon

Blend cream cheese and condensed milk, add eggs and cream and mix until smooth, add vanilla and lemon juice. Rest in fridge for 4 hours

Pour onto pastry and bake 130c for 1 hour until set.
Check by tapping the sides, it is ready when it wobbles like jelly.

Whisk 200mls sour cream and 25g sugar, pour this over the cheesecake, spread evenly and bake for a further 10 minutes.
Cool the cake and serve.

Baked Cheesecake with ricotta

Base
¾ cup flour
1/3 cup ground almonds
¼ cup caster sugar
90 g butter

Rub butter and dry ingredients altogether, mix until breadcrumb consistency, pour into cake tin 20cm spread out and press into tin base with the back of a spoon.
Bake 150c until just golden.

Filling
Put all ingredients into a processor
500g ricotta
330g chopped cream cheese
4 eggs
1⅓ cup castor sugar
¼ cup lemon juice
2 tablespoons lemon zest
1 teaspoon vanilla essence
1½ tablespoons water mixed with 1½ tablespoons Cornflour

Whiz altogether
Grease the sides of pastry base cake tin, pour in filling.
Slightly tap tin to release bubbles. Use a back of a spoon to smooth out the bubbles.
Bake 150c for 1 hour.
Turn off oven and leave in oven until cool.
Refrigerate before serving.

Bake cheesecake with raspberry sauce

250g plain biscuits
½ teaspoon ground cinnamon
60g butter, melted
500g cream cheese, at room temperature
2 tablespoons plain flour
¼ teaspoon salt
270g caster sugar
125g sour cream
1 tablespoon vanilla extract
3 eggs, at room temperature
Mixed fresh berries and icing sugar, to serve

Preheat oven to 160C.
Lightly grease a 20cm round spring form cake pan. Line the base with baking paper.
Process biscuits in a food processor until finely crushed.
Add cinnamon and butter, then process until mixture resembles wet sand.
Pour mixture into prepared pan and press over base and 4cm up the side. Refrigerate.
Cream the Cream cheese until soft and fluffy.
Beat in flour and salt.
Beat in sugar, sour cream and vanilla until well combined.
Beat in eggs, one at a time, until just combined.
Pour mixture over biscuit base.

Bake for 45 minutes or until just set, but still has a slight wobble in the centre. Turn off oven and open door about 10 cm. Cool the cheesecake in the oven, then refrigerate for 4 hours or overnight.

Raspberry sauce
To make raspberry sauce, mash raspberries and sugar in a saucepan over medium heat until soft and broken down. Pass through a fine sieve. Refrigerate until cold. You can replace the raspberries with any other berries.

3 cups frozen raspberries
75g icing sugar
Serve drizzled over the cheesecake.

Fresh cherry cheesecake

3 cups ricotta cheese
100mls sour cream
4 large eggs separated
¾ cup castor sugar
I teaspoon vanilla essence
1 tablespoon lemon zest
1 cup fresh cherries
Icing sugar

Butter and flour 18-20 cm spring form cake tin
In food processor blend together ricotta and sour cream, until smooth.
Add egg yolks, ¼ cup sugar, vanilla and zest.
Lightly process to combine, transfer to a large bowl.
Fold in the fresh cherries.

Beat egg whites gradually add the ½ cup sugar, beat.
Fold ¼ of the egg whites into the cheese cherry mixture.
Add the remaining egg white and fold, until no egg whites are visible.

Pour into tin.
Bake 150c for about 1 hour 15 minutes, until the cheesecake has risen but still pale on top.
Remove from tin and dredge with icing sugar

Chili lime cheesecake

1 packet ginger nuts or super wine biscuits
125g melted butter
1 teaspoon cinnamon

Blender the biscuits until a fine crumb, add in the cinnamon and pour in the butter, press into spring tin, chill

250kg cream cheese
1 tin condensed milk
2 fresh de seeded chilies chopped finely
Cream the cream cheese with the condensed milk then add in
½ cup lemon juice
½ cup lime juice
2 teaspoon gelatin dissolved in ½ cup hot water

Mix altogether, and then fold in 500ml whipped cream.
Refrigerate until set.
Serve with sweet chili sauce.

(This dessert was the overall winner in the Montana wine and food challenge award, which was to match the wine with the dessert, an outstanding wine match)

Dairy Products

Mascarpone

1litre cream
1/2 teaspoon tartaric acid

To make mascarpone, scald cream and tartaric acid. Cool overnight, Line a fine sieve with damp muslin or clean chux cloth. Pour mixture into lined sieve and drain 24 hours in fridge, turning edges to middle occasionally.
Makes 500mls of mascarpone.

Cream Fraiche

500ml cream
250ml buttermilk or sour cream

Heat gently until just below body temp, 25c.
Pour cream into a container and partly cover it.
Keep at this temp for 6-8 hours or until it has thickened and tastes slightly acid. The cream will thicken faster on a hot day. Stir and store in fridge for up to 2 weeks.
Makes 750ml.

Ricotta cheese

Heat 2 litres of whole milk slowly in double boiler to 80-90 degrees c
Add ¼ cup white vinegar while and **very /very** slowly stirring.
Stop stirring once curds have formed.
Gently scoop into a lined colander and cool quickly to let curd set.
May be used straight away.
Very means very slowly, it is cutting through the milk to form the curds.

Cottage Cheese

1 litre milk
2 teaspoons rennet

Heat milk to lukewarm and remove from heat. Add rennet, stir slowly for thirty seconds, and allow setting.
Break up the curd and put it into a sieve lined with muslin or a Chux cloth. Stand overnight to separate the curds and whey. Place in a clean container; it can be used immediately or stored in the refrigerator.

Sour Cream (1)

1 cup cream
¼ cup of original sour cream culture or buttermilk

Put all ingredients into a screw-top jar and stand at room temperature for 24 hours until thick. Refrigerate.
Note: Buttermilk is a by-product of butter-making. It freezes and can be used for cooking.

Sour Cream (2)

1 cup cream
1 tablespoon buttermilk

Recipe can be increased at the ratio of 1 tablespoon buttermilk to 1 cup of cream.
In a double boiler bring the fresh cream up to 180 degrees.
Take of the pot and cool to room temp.
Add the buttermilk, cover, and let sit at room temperature. For 24-48 hours. Stir and refrigerate.
The batch will keep approximately 3-4 weeks, refrigerated.

Sour Cream (3)

1 cup cream
1½ cups pasteurized whole milk
½ cup buttermilk

Mix all the ingredients in a bowl over warm water or in a double boiler. Raise the temperature of the mixture to (68 degrees to 70 degrees F) and let it stand for 12 to 24 hours or until it is sufficiently sour and thick enough to cling firmly to a spoon.
Keep in the refrigerator until you want to use it. For a richer heavier sour cream combine 2 cups of pasteurized heavy cream with 5 tablespoons of cultured buttermilk and incubate as before. For better texture refrigerate for 24 hours before serving.

Tips and Hints on Using Sour Cream
Sour cream is commonly used for dips, dressings, and sauces or simply "plain" as a condiment.
Never boil sour cream because it will curdle immediately. To add sour cream to a hot liquid, remove the liquid from the heat source (or turn the heat to very low) and add the cream while stirring gently. Avoid using sour cream in dishes with a lot of salt, as the salt may cause curdling. Also, dishes made with sour cream do not freeze well

Baking with Sour Cream
Cakes using acidic ingredients such as sour cream may development a metallic flavor if baked and stored in an aluminum pan. To prevent this reaction from taking place, line the bottom of the pan with parchment paper before adding the batter to the pan.

Sour Cream Dip

1 cup or 250g sour cream
Salt and pepper to taste.

Chopped herbs of your choice: chives, coriander, tarragon, dill, spring onions: you may want to add calendula petals for character.

Buttermilk from soy milk or milk

1 cup milk or soy milk add 1 tablespoon vinegar or lemon juice to the milk it will curdle use it all.

Rennet

Liquid vegetarian rennet can be made from stinging nettle or whole dandelion plant and flowers. Put a large bunch in a pot, cover and bring to boil. Leave to cool for 2 hours and use a tablespoon of the liquid.
Rennet also comes from the white sap of figs, lemon juice, white vinegar, citric acid. These can all be used in cheese-making, though they will not make a hard cheese. For that, you'll need commercial rennet.

Mild feta cheese

4 ½ litres milk
¼ cup cheese culture or buttermilk
½ teaspoon liquid rennet
¼ cup cool water
Coarse salt

Warm milk to 86° F and stir in cheese culture or buttermilk.
Set one hour to ripen.
Mix rennet into cool water and stir into milk.
Cover and allow setting another hour to coagulate.
Cut curds into 2 cm cubes and allow to rest five minutes. Stir gently for 15 minutes, keeping the curds at 86 degrees (put pot in a basin of hot water).
Pour curds into a cheesecloth-lined colander, tie the bag of curds and hang to drain for four to six hours.
Slice the cheese ball in half and lay the slabs of cheese into a dish that can be covered.
Sprinkle all the surfaces with coarse salt, cover and allow setting at room temperature for 24 hours.
After 24 hours, salt all the surfaces with more coarse salt and let it rest for two hours.
Place the cheese in a covered dish and refrigerate for five to seven days.
Use within two weeks or freeze for future use. The cheese will keep at room temperature for months if marinated in oil.

Yoghurt

1 litre milk; any kind
3 Tablespoons non-fat dried milk powder (optional)
Starter: 2 tablespoons existing yogurt with live cultures,
i.e. natural yogurt or acidophilus yogurt.

Whisk milk powder into a little of the milk until completely dissolved; this will help thicken the yoghurt more easily and add more nutrition.
Then add the rest of milk and stir.
Heat the milk until it starts to froth, or the temperature reaches 85C. Do not boil or burn the milk. Microwaving is good: it takes 8 to 10 minutes on high, depending on the microwave wattage.
Cool the milk to room temperature or baby-milk temperature.
Add the starter yoghurt to the cooled milk.
Keep the yoghurt warm in either a yoghurt maker or an Easy-Yo container.
Or you could use an oven where the temperature is maintained at 38C (having the oven light on might be enough); or in a double boiler - or maybe put it in your car on a sunny day. Just use your common sense and a thermometer.
After 8 hours the yoghurt should have a thickish appearance, and the whey - a thin yellow liquid - will form on top.
You can pour off the whey or stir into yoghurt.
Refrigerated, this yoghurt will keep for 1 to 2 weeks.
Use 2 tablespoons of this yoghurt to create the next yoghurt within 5 days to keep the bacteria growing.

Yoghurt Cream Cheese

1kg plain yoghurt
Put yoghurt in a sieve lined with muslin or a Chux cloth, place over a bowl, and leave in the fridge for about 1 to 2 days to drain. Once drained place in clean containers.
The drained liquid is called whey and the solid part is called curds. Have the curds as plain cream cheese, or add herbs, spices, jams, fresh fruit and nuts to create a tasty cheese spread. Whey is full of amazing enzymes: add it to your soup, pikelets, pancakes, and muffins.

Yoghurt Ice blocks

Place yoghurt into small plastic cup containers or ice block containers. Pureed fruit or chopped fruit can be added to the yogurt to make fruit-filled yogurt blocks.
To centre the all-important popsicle stick, place tin foil over container and poke popsicle stick through the middle. Freeze.

Condiments - Hints

Almond milk

1 cup raw almonds soak in 1 cup water and take of skin.
Place almonds in blender and add 3 cups water and whizz until smooth.
Strain in cloth and store in fridge for 3-4 days.

Baking powder mix

2 teaspoons cream of tartar
1 teaspoon baking soda,
1 teaspoon cornstarch

Egg replacer

1 tablespoon white vinegar for each egg

Gluten Flour Mix

1 ½ cups millet flour
1 ½ cups sorghum flour
1 cup tapioca flour
1 cup potato starch
1 cup arrowroot powder

Rice flour mix

5 ½ cups brown rice flour
1 ½ cups potato starch
1 cup tapioca starch
Variation: replace 2 cups brown rice flour with
equal amount of almond meal, chickpea/ garbanzo bean flour
or garfava bean flour.

More Inspiring Books by the Author

'Back to Basics'

This book focuses on inspiring the reader to examine alternatives to expensive chemical-based products. Discover how our common weeds are power-packed full of nutritional and medicinal healing. Learn to match the herb with the dish: which herbs to use in cooking. Learn how to make medicinal tinctures, poultice and herbal infusions. Have fun making natural alternatives for health, beauty and body products. Learn how to make mascarpone, sour cream, and ricotta. Have fun with these home recipes; you'll discover a new way to wellbeing.

'Back to Basics Harvest'

161 recipes for creating chutneys, jams, vinaigrettes, sauces and jellies, just the way your grandmother used to, in the days when all good food was created in the home kitchen. Suzanne Massee is passionate about home-grown and home-produced foods; her home-produced preserves have been sold throughout New Zealand.
Suzanne's restaurant was winner of the 2003 Wine and Food Challenge Award for Nelson-Marlborough – West Coast Region.
The author says "My passion is the study of natural products – I love to teach others about what is around us all. It's time for me to share these wonderful recipes: instead of just keeping them in the computer, it has come time to put them all on paper. Let me teach you, your children and grandchildren the art of preserving, so that you can know that what you are consuming, is full of goodness and wholeness."
This book is the outcome of years spent accumulating recipes, in a format that makes it easier to make the most of each season's harvests.

'Clarity'

Clarity is lining up with something that is really clear, and I like it, it makes me feel good. Clarity is in the transformation of the contrast into better feeling thoughts, not to avoid the negative thoughts but to transform and emphasis new better thoughts which makes me feel good.
The Law of Attraction says; nothing comes without your attention to it, and nothing stays without your attention to it.
You are bringing the reality in, of which is in your imagination of what you want, in other words reality does not exist, it is the thoughts that bring about the reality. Reality only exists if you keep on perpetuating it. Reality then becomes the wanted or unwanted desires
The true sign of intelligence is not knowledge but imagination: Albert Einstein
A belief is only a thought you keep thinking, if it feels good than you are in alignment with your Inner Being, if you feel angst or not feeling good, it is you separating you from your Inner Being, your Inner Being is not following you on this belief thought.
Simply co-creating at its best - all the abundance - all the wants - all the dreams - all the desires, are amassing in your vibrational escrow. It is simply the laws of the universe that make the desires become into beingness.

'Amplify Thoughts'

Everything is thought. You will discover your mind is thought and every thought is creation, your thoughts can be inspiring, exhilarating, joyful, happy, in love with life, and what it has to offer, this is pure connection to your well-being, your worthiness.
Or your thoughts may be subdued apprehensive, fear based, or negative connotations; this is not connection to your well-being, but an indicator that your thoughts are pointing you in the wrong direction.
To increase the momentum of uplifting thoughts is to inspire the feeling within; welcome to Amplifying Thoughts and discover feelings and emotions.
Amplify and build up momentum to inspiring thoughts, this is the way to communicate with your greater part of you, your Inner Being, which is the Source of you.

'Conversations with Consciousness'

Vibrational frequency energy: is the transference of energy from one object to another or converted into form, very much disbelieved unless they can see it or touch.
If conceivable and all the humans which populate this earth, were to realise they are all transmitting mechanisms, and have this powerful signal which is never detached from them and is holding every desire you wish to become a reality, wouldn't you really like to tap into this resourceful guidance system.
Wouldn't it be nicer to live in your desires. Drive your desires – work in your desires – play in your desires – have the best relationships;
Welcome! You have just made the best decision to broaden your perspective and the continuing motion forward in the stimulation of thought.

'Thoughts Create'

This is who you really are;
You are a vortex of energy residing in a physical house to expand your consciousness which is eternal.
You were eager to play the dance and to remember your vortex of energy.
This vortex of energy knows what you desire and when you want to leave this physical house and how.
You knew you could tap into this stream of energy and create with your thoughts and emotions to communicate with your vortex, you knew you could imagine whatever you wanted to be and do, and you knew you could trust the process and your vortex of energy will orchestrate the event.
You are the beholder of your thoughts.
Look at your thoughts, and you will discover everything that you are living is created by you, and not by anyone else.
These powerful thoughts are created by you, and to every thought there is an opposite, and with every thought is followed by an emotion.
Makes you kind of want to think about what you are thinking about.

Social media

https://www.suzannemassee.com

https://www.amazon.com/-/e/B00DFBFRJK

https://suzannemassee782038939.wordpress.com/blog/

https://www.facebook.com/massee19/

https://www.smashwords.com/profile/view/suzannemassee

https://www.instagram.com/suzanne.massee/

https://www.facebook.com/suzannem19/

The Author

I had a cafeteria where I created the most delicious slices, the compliment of these slice recipes was through my father in-law who was the general manager and baker for a very popular bakery in Timaru in the South Island of New Zealand. These slice recipes have been handed down, and I have reduced the ingredient measurements from very large baker's trays to the household trays.

My passion is my love of natural products - and teaching others about what is around us all. This brought about my first book "Back to Basics" and now this follow-up, "Back to Basics Harvest" These books came about from my experience while in the restaurant business, and with the arrange of preserves and Christmas cakes which were made and sold throughout New Zealand.

I was just an ordinary person, living a normal existence ... or so I thought ... until I had a near-death experience in a head-on car collision, after the opposing driver fell asleep. This accident catapulted me onto an incredible journey. Through all this, I found my way onto the solid road of the inner spirit; one's very own path to understanding and opening to one's inner consciousness. I delight in teaching others "to harvest the self": that a correct relationship with oneself is of primary importance. From this can flow correct relationships with others and trust in the divine source. Further readings on who we really are available 'Clarity' 'Adam and Eve Becoming' and 'Amplify Thoughts'

Contents

Introduction	4
Baking	6
Chocolate Brownie	6
Chocolate Brownie (2)	7
Chocolate Cake	8
Carrot Cake	9
Lemon poppy seed cake	10
Sponge	11
Friands	12
Boiled fruit cake	13
Chocolate zucchini cake	14
Orange almond cake	15
Orange and lemon cake	16
Semolina cake	17
Rhubarb cake	18
Moist Chocolate Genoese for wedding cakes	19
Truffles	21
Mint Truffles	21
Fruit and nut balls (1)	22
Fruit and nut balls (2)	23
Pastry	24
Hot water pastry	24
Short pastry	25
Yummy quick pastry	25
Puff Pastry	26
Crumpets	26
Quinoa quiche crust	27
Quiche pastry	27
Quiche fillings	28
Wonton wrappers	29
Dumpling wrappers	29
Steam buns	29
Icings – Fillings	30
Caramel	31
Plain icing	32
Chocolate icing	32
Cream cheese icing	32
Slices	34
Tan squares	34
Sultana squares or Apple slice.	34
Apple strudel	35
Jumble	35
Fudge	36
Ginger slice	36
Peanut slice	37
Churchill square	38
Coconut Ice slice	39
Rocky road	39
Russian slice	40
Peppermint slice	40
Belgium slice	41
Rock melon slice	42
Coconut crumble	43
Coconut macaroon	43
Mums biscuits	45
Anzac biscuits	45
Kiwi biscuits	46
Lolly cake	46
Mays shortbread	47
Deluxe shortbread	47
Lavosh Crackers	48
Sugar buns	50
Scones	50
Muffins	51
Coconut bread	52
Olliebollen Donuts (Dutch doughnut)	53
Pikelets	54
Christmas cake	56
Jewel cake	57
Gluten Free Bread	59
Spelt biscuits	60
Spelt bread	60
Spelt bread 2	61
Gluten Free Vegan Bread	62
Gluten Flour Mix	62
Multi-grain bread	63
Sago Plum Pudding	65
Sticky date pudding	66
Apple Crumble	67
Individual steamed puddings	68
Golden winter pudding	69
Steam Pudding	70
Christmas Steamed pudding	71
Anglaise custard and Brandy cream	72
Frangipane Tart	73
The ultimate chocolate mousse	75
Chocolate mousse in minutes	75
Butter scotch whip	75
Toffee Sauce	75
Caramel Sauce	75
Crème Brule	76
Meringues with Kaffir lime syrup and fruit	76
Chocolate truffle cake with raspberry sauce	77
Baked Cheesecake with sour cream topping	78
Baked Cheesecake with ricotta	79
Bake cheesecake with raspberry sauce	80
Fresh cherry cheesecake	81
Chili lime cheesecake	82
Mascarpone	84
Cream Fraiche	84
Ricotta cheese	84
Cottage Cheese	84
Sour Cream (1)	85
Sour Cream (2)	85
Sour Cream (3)	85
Sour Cream Dip	86
Buttermilk from soy milk or milk	86
Rennet	86
Mild feta cheese	86
Yoghurt	87
Yoghurt Cream Cheese	87
Yoghurt Ice blocks	87
Almond milk	88
Baking powder mix	88
Egg replacer	88
Gluten Flour Mix	88
Rice flour mix	88
Author	94

www.ingramcontent.com/pod-product-compliance
Lightning Source LLC
Chambersburg PA
CBHW082244300426
44110CB00036B/2444